★★★★★★THE
TUESDAY CABINET
Deliberation
and Decision
on Peace and War
under Lyndon B. Johnson

Books by Henry F. Graff

Bluejackets with Perry in Japan
The Modern Researcher (with Jacques Barzun)
The Adventure of the American People
  (with John A. Krout)
The Free and the Brave
American Imperialism and the Philippine Insurrection

THE
TUESDAY CABINET

Deliberation

and Decision

on Peace and War

under Lyndon B. Johnson

by Henry F. Graff

☆☆☆☆☆☆

PRENTICE-HALL, INC.
Englewood Cliffs, N. J.

THE TUESDAY CABINET
Deliberation and Decision on Peace and War
under Lyndon B. Johnson
by Henry F. Graff
© 1970 by Henry F. Graff

Library of Congress Catalog Card Number: 70–117947
Printed in the United States of America • *T*

JUL 10 '72

ISBN 0–13–932582–4
Prentice-Hall International, Inc., London
Prentice-Hall of Australia, Pty. Ltd., Sydney
Prentice-Hall of Canada, Ltd., Toronto
Prentice-Hall of India Private Ltd., New Delhi
Prentice-Hall of Japan, Inc., Tokyo

Acknowledgments

I RECOGNIZE, ABOVE ALL, A HEAVY DEBT OF GRATITUDE TO
President Johnson and the members of the Tuesday Cabinet,
as well as others who come up in this narrative, for having
given me so generously of their time and best thought at
momentous junctures in the nation's career.

To a number of colleagues and other friends who prof-
fered me indispensable help of various kinds, my sense of
obligation is also very great. If they should read this book
they will know of my lasting appreciation.

For permission to use—albeit in considerably altered form
—material of mine originally published in *The New York
Times Magazine,* I thank the New York Times Company.
And I am obliged to *The New York Times* and *Life* magazine for making available to me White House and other
photographs in their collections.

To E.K.G., I.J.G., and E.T.G.

Contents

INTRODUCTION

DURING THE PRESIDENCY OF LYNDON JOHNSON, TUESDAY WAS a special day. Each week, almost without exception, the President and his senior advisers gathered for lunch and deliberation in the President's Dining Room on the second floor of the White House. The agenda was unvarying: the war in Vietnam and the related questions that that intractable topic generated.

Anyone who wants to weigh the reasons for American participation in the war or to make concrete the abstraction called Presidential leadership, dare not overlook those weekly luncheon meetings. There the key men of the Republic proposed, analyzed, and argued about the policies that were to be associated forever with the name of the Chief. There they struggled to learn "the other side's" short-run intentions— having concluded decisively about the long-range ones. There they shared their hesitations and anxieties, discussed and often impugned the motives of their domestic opponents, shaped the Administration's verbal defenses, and searched for the historical precedents to rely on for comfort and support.

The composition of the Tuesday Cabinet changed from time to time but its work was distinctively continuous because new men joined it only infrequently and always one at a time. The members, when the meetings began early in 1965, were Dean Rusk, the Secretary of State; Robert S. McNamara, the Secretary of Defense; and McGeorge Bundy, Special Assistant to the President for National Security Affairs. (Facetious journalists in Washington sometimes referred to these men and the President collectively as the "awesome foursome.") Not long after the first meetings were held, Bill D. Moyers, who was Special Assistant to the President and who had recently become White House Press Secretary, joined the original group. In inviting Moyers the President was meeting the need he felt to have at the table someone not tied bureaucratically to existing policies and with whom he could afterward weigh the purport of the sessions.

In the early days of the Tuesday Cabinet, General Earle G. Wheeler, the Chairman of the Joint Chiefs of Staff, was invited only on an *ad hoc* basis. After the beginning of 1966 he was usually present, because the President responded to two pressures: the objections that the uniformed services registered privately over not being fully represented at these meetings, and the growing conviction in the Administration that regrettably the solution to the Vietnam problem was going to be military rather than diplomatic. At about the same time and for comparable reasons, Richard M. Helms, the Director of the Central Intelligence Agency, also began to be invited.*

After McGeorge Bundy left the White House in 1966, Walt W. Rostow, his successor, took his place at the lunches. In similar fashion George E. Christian, who succeeded Moyers in 1966, and Clark M. Clifford, who succeeded McNamara in 1968, inherited seats at the table. Occasionally the President invited trusted consultants not in official life or people with particular expertness to join the luncheon-group.

In 1965, through special circumstances I shall shortly relate, I began to have conversations with some of these men and became aware of the historic importance of their meetings which were then generally unknown to the larger public. Being by profession an historian and having no official

---

* For biographical information on the members of the group see Appendix A.

or private connection with the Administration, I used these conversations as occasions to study at firsthand how a President reaches his decisions; how Johnson, notably, made his decisions about Vietnam. Most of the scenario for the conduct of the war, I quickly discovered, was written on Tuesdays.

The grand room in which the Tuesday Cabinet met was the President's choice—for reasons he may never have formulated to himself. It was the room the family ate in, and as such the inner sanctum of the Presidency. There the First Family could be private together and safely speak their spontaneous thoughts about state or other matters. For anyone not a member of the family to take a meal there was a privilege that only a handful of people had ever enjoyed. One may think it bespoke a sense of obligation in the host for him to issue a standing invitation to lunch in this room, a sense matched by the guest's feelings, each week reinforced, of being a trusted, loyal intimate. Was there, too, an atmosphere in the appointments of the room itself that affected the participants? When their attention wandered, as occasionally must have happened, their eyes would rest on brilliant panels of wallpaper depicting American soldiers of the Revolutionary War in the glorious moments of victory at Yorktown and elsewhere—as if to mock the subject of their own war councils.

On one question there is no uncertainty. Johnson's Tuesday Cabinet left its mark on the history of the United States as ineradicably as Jackson's Kitchen Cabinet or Theodore Roosevelt's Tennis Cabinet or Franklin Roosevelt's Brain Trust. And considering the impact of its discussions on the rest of the world, the Tuesday Cabinet is in a category alone. Its members sometimes gathered at other times than at the noon hour on Tuesdays and at various places in and away from the White House, for war does not respect fixed schedules. Nevertheless, most explicitly, Tuesday was the day set aside for the President by the advisers he depended upon most. Reports from Vietnam, fresh proposals for action (including the designation of bombing targets), suggestions of new representations to be tried on the diplomatic front—such was the standard fare. On Tuesday, if no new crisis had intervened, the style of the Administration showed itself: members displayed the stature of their intellects and competed for the attention and favor of their Chief. Their very presence at that exquisite Sheraton dining table was the reward of the opportunity attached to holding the highest offices in the land.

The men of the Tuesday Cabinet were loyal to each other, with a devotion compounded of mutual respect and common adversity. They soon learned, as all congenial committeemen learn, to listen selectively and to talk harmoniously even when in disagreement. Familiarity with one another's minds became an asset as well as a handicap in the years they conferred and labored. And their facility with words (laced with the Pentagonese all spoke so fluently) made the sessions memorable for the participants week in and week out—even as the uncertainty of the President's mood would heighten the tension.

Anything like a full account of the meetings of the Tuesday Cabinet would entail formidable research. There are virtually no records, because the type of gathering precluded the keeping of formal minutes. From 1967 on some notes were taken of important statements and memoranda to be prepared; of documents to be circulated and people to be telephoned; but no transcripts were made of the conversations themselves. The value of the discussions would have been ruined by formal procedures.

Still, the discussions of the Tuesday Cabinet being an integral part of American history, is it possible to find out what they were like? The unique confluence of people, moods, ideas, facts, sensitivities, and pressures each week cannot be brought back to life: the tone and tint were inevitably fleeting. How the participants felt right then about their Chief, their colleagues, even themselves—to say nothing of the besetting problems at hand; why they believed what they said they believed—all this evanescent reality could have been discerned, if at all, only by an omniscient witness in the heat of the event.

To be sure, the high moments could have been recorded *physically* on film and tape like any other high table conversation. But this too would be inadequate, even falsifying. Argument is composed of more complex ingredients than what is spoken, and the inhibiting presence of machinery would have changed the chemistry by which they combined. The Tuesday Cabinet would have been transformed into a stage and perhaps deformed by its theatrics.

Again, one might have tried to record as soon as possible after each meeting the words of the members, explaining the stand each took on crucial matters and the degree of influence he brought to bear on his colleagues. Here too, the artificiality is plain: discourses, monologues, would replace the rapid give-and-take across the table which was the actuality of the occasion.

A last stratagem would have been for an historian to put questions from time to time to the members of the Tuesday Cabinet and coax from each an explanation or amplification of his stand. The historian might of course have failed to ask the right questions, or he might have skewed the distribution of his time: he, like them, could be trapped by the mood of the moment.

And yet, for the particular historian and his readers, such an arrangement could prove invaluable. He could catch the nuances of verbal and facial expression, intuit the physical and historical setting in which decisions grew, carry points and queries from one participant to another; in short, he could probe as well as converse. He would not presume to guess what future generations might want to know about the Tuesday Cabinet, but he would place at their disposal his trained perspective and his developed sense of the proportion of events.

At four critical moments in the history of the Vietnam War between 1965 and 1968, I had the privilege and satisfaction of being that questioning historian. No one—I least of all—could have foretold the importance of the particular occasions on which I was present. The White House simply invited me each time to have conversations with President Johnson and members of the Tuesday Cabinet* about their stewardship of foreign policy. I was left free to make whatever notes I cared to and either to write them up for publication fairly soon or put them in the deep-freeze of posthumous papers for much later publication.

The circumstances that led to the invitation date back to the Spring of 1965. Members of the White House staff (I later learned) shared the President's concern that the public was largely unaware of his ability to handle international affairs; it appeared to think that his political skill stopped at the water's edge. But the President and his aides had concluded otherwise, especially after his performance in defusing the controversial question of a multilateral nuclear force staffed by the NATO nations.

The initiative to invite me to write about the President's handling of international affairs came from E. Hayes Redmon, then serving as assistant to Bill Moyers. Redmon, who later had the title of Staff Assistant to the President, was a popular figure in Great Society Washington. Through his hands passed the results of the public-opinion polls on their way to the President and he helped prepare the President's legislative program for 1965. A graduate of the United States Naval Academy, Redmon attended Columbia University

---

* The name is mine; the White House always referred to the "Tuesday lunch."

from 1958 to 1960 and received the M.A. degree in history. I first met him at that time, when he was a student in my graduate course on the History of the Foreign Relations of the United States. Redmon, an indefatigable student of American politics, possessed, in addition to a lively mind, an unusual love of history.

Spurred by Redmon, Moyers concluded that an historian rather than a journalist was required to converse with Lyndon Johnson about foreign policy. Because an historian of diplomacy was preferred, it came about that I was offered this extraordinary opportunity. On my side, nothing had led to suspect that such an invitation was in the offing. The phone call from Moyers' office took me completely by surprise.

I accepted and from the outset was aware that the interest of the White House and mine touched at many points though they were far from parallel or complementary. Both sides were clear that no political service or allegiance was involved. My interest was that of a student of contemporary history. By 1965 when the American people were beginning to perceive the terrible dilemmas of the Vietnam involvement, I was pondering and scrutinizing the problems of Presidential leadership—in particular the problem of how the United States could avoid being the world's policeman while shouldering its duties in international politics. I had shortly before published in *The New York Times Magazine* an article entitled "Isolation Again—with a Difference," * in which I had decried the apparent reassertion of isolationist sentiment among Americans as a result of the frustrations caused by the war in Vietnam and the dispatching of troops to the Dominican Republic.

I had never written on the subject of the war itself. To prepare for my White House conversations, I briefed myself anew on the intricate history of the conflict, and especially

* May 4, 1965, © 1965 by The New York Times Company.

on the role and position of President Johnson and of the men around him. Meanwhile in Washington, Moyers and Redmon were arranging a schedule of appointments, having asked me whom I wanted to see. It was my fortune to arrive in the capital for the first of my talks with the President during the very week in June, 1965 when the decision was about to be made to increase significantly the number of American troops in Vietnam.

Early in 1966, the White House invited me to pursue the discussion with the leaders of the Administration. (The President, I was told, had said shortly after my first visit, "We must have him back again.") The second time my conversations followed President Johnson's return from Honolulu, where he had met Premier Nguyen Cao Ky for the first time, and discussed plans for post-war reconstruction in South Vietnam.

Moyers resigned from his White House post soon afterward, but he kept up his interest in my meetings. From New York in the late Fall of 1967, Moyers was in touch with George Christian, his successor as Press Secretary, and encouraged him to urge upon the President another round of these conversations. The result was that with Christian's more than willing aid, I saw the President and his advisers again just before the Tet Offensive at the beginning of 1968. In November of that year, Christian invited me once again, when the White House was still reverberating from the decision to halt the bombing of North Vietnam. The Administration was by then running out of time and the transition to President Nixon's day was well-advanced.

Before or after each of my talks with the President except the last, I talked at length also with his principal advisers—the members of the Tuesday Cabinet. I saw each in his own office; I did not see exactly the same group of men each time. Always with their permission I took copious notes, bearing in mind the ease with which even weighty words can become distorted by relying on the memory alone after the passage of time, however short. I filled in my notes as soon as I had returned to my hotel room, taking advantage of the knack that historians cultivate, of recalling details in quantity and often verbatim after instructive conversation or reading.

It only dawned on me after the first of these conversations that the record I hoped to compile would be unprecedented in Presidential historiography: a presentation and defense of an Administration's war aims to an historian by the men responsible for framing and implementing them, including the President himself. In our later talks, I twice mentioned to President Johnson that no previous war president—Jefferson, Madison, Polk, Lincoln, McKinley, the two Roosevelts, Wilson, or Truman—had talked on a planned basis in similar fashion about the war he was conducting. When I tried to draw out the President's thoughts on the significance he attached to these conversations, including the access he was giving me to his chief aides, he responded only silently and with a grin that I could not but regard as indicating gratification.

The President knew I was going to write about the meetings, but we never talked about where or when—nor referred to the form the writing would take. Each time, however, the White House Press Office knew that I had a "first refusal" agreement with *The New York Times*. A long article based on the first set of conversations appeared shortly afterward in *The New York Times Magazine.**

A shorter article growing out of the second set of conversations was also published in *The New York Times Magazine.*** A third was written for the same magazine about

* July 4, 1965, under the title "How Johnson Makes Foreign Policy." A portion of the article was published on the same day in *The Sunday Times* (London). © 1965 by The New York Times Company.
** March 20, 1966, under the title "Teach-in on Vietnam—by the President, the Secretary of State, the Secretary of Defense, and the Under Secretary of State." © 1966 by The New York Times Company.

11

the third series, but the *Pueblo* affair and the Tet Offensive intervened and after these, in the opinion of the editors, the article no longer had the immediacy of news.

When I had finished the first and second articles, I sent a copy to Bill Moyers and Hayes Redmon and *The New York Times Magazine* simultaneously. Moyers and Redmon, as we had agreed, cleared the direct quotations. All the quotations in the third article were cleared by W. Thomas Johnson, the Assistant Press Secretary, at George Christian's direction, except those of Secretary McNamara, which were cleared by Mr. McNamara's office.

Clearance was each time conducted over the telephone between myself and the persons concerned, and clearance bore solely on direct quotations. I did not consider that this arrangement, informally carried out, was too high a price to pay for the chance to put on record as soon as could be the views of members of the Tuesday Cabinet. At no time did we ever talk beforehand about what could or could not be discussed or afterward published. The very few changes requested were trifling: they related only to what the President had said and only to his phrasing, not to the substance. Secretaries Rusk and McNamara both said they were satisfied to have Moyers clear their remarks for direct quotation. But this deference to Moyers' judgment should not be taken to mean that they were casual about their words or about the possible political or security implications of carelessness. On one occasion Secretary McNamara broke the thread of our conversation to refresh his mind about what he called "the ground rules" for our conversation, saying to me (as if I did not fully realize it): "You know this will be read in Peking."

The substance of the present book is considerably different and richer than the contents of my two published articles. It is a complete account of the conversations I had with the President and his senior aides as these conversations were written down from my notes immediately after they took place. I have edited the text only lightly, and solely for greater clarity and ease of reading. The two articles that appeared in the *Times Magazine* could obviously not contain the detail published here. Moreover, some matters that were politically sensitive when they were uttered are now innocuous. Security was probably never at issue and is certainly not involved today, either in the first two Parts or in the last two, which are published here for the first time. In conformity with the spirit of the original plan to capture permanently a sense of how President Johnson and his men talked about their central problem, I have used their own words, unvarnished, as I heard them.

The men of the Tuesday Cabinet were masterful figures, but the overwhelming force in their official lives was Lyndon Baines Johnson. To the end he held them privately bound and publicly loyal. Only they can report what it was like to be in his service. To me, he always seemed to strain more under the burden of the Presidency than his predecessors, whose manner and style I admit I know almost entirely from books alone. The explanation no doubt lay deep in the wellsprings of his personality, for he had always borne the weight of office heavily, almost as if he wished upon himself the responsibility of power as an exercise in endurance.

Like all successful politicians, Johnson longed to do what was right, even when "right" arose not out of an impulse felt personally and viscerally but out of consultation with colleagues and friends. Johnson made gigantic demands upon himself to achieve great things, and it was easy to see that his self-punishment was mental as well as physical. Because his main business in the White House was to make decisions and to create the political climate in which they would be accepted, he occupied himself almost solely in manipulating the delicate and balky machinery of power.

13

Nevertheless, he performed the work self-consciously, as if it did not come as easily to him as most of his countrymen assumed it did. He illustrated this generality in a number of dramatic ways: his incessant and sometimes pretentious citing of the reports of public-opinion polls; his frequent references in public utterances to himself as "your President" —as though he had to reassure himself as well as his hearers; and his need to have a ubiquitous cameraman at work, turning every moment of the Johnson Presidency into a visible fact.

Being a patriot as well as a President, Johnson was jealous of his reputation in the history books, which for him meant at first his place in the affections of his countrymen. As the years rolled on, he appeared ready to settle for their respect. Inevitably, he became dependent on history to vindicate him by applauding his policies and the stamina that he displayed against stubborn, "wrong-headed" opponents.

Only Presidents can say to what extent in their fantasies they see themselves first crucified by their fellow-Americans, and then risen again on the future coins and postage stamps of the United States. All Presidents no doubt wind up as suppliants before posterity. Johnson felt as keenly as any of his predecessors that chief among the wages of power is the judgment of tomorrow, and that every moment of his increasingly stormy Administration was going to be a plaything of historians. Johnson, in other words, was alternately attracted and repelled by historians and their enterprise, aware that he could not ignore or escape them. The documentary accumulation of his five years in the White House is the Mount Everest among the collections of Presidential papers. It testifies to his concern about his public repute as well as to the wide range of his work.

No one can say for sure whether Johnson was more given to "making the record" on his own decisions than other Chief Executives have been. He was interested in history for its own sake, to be sure, but primarily, it seemed to me, for his own place in it. Not being a reader of books, history to him was portraits and memorials of the kind that had surrounded him throughout his public life. I recall that at a brief ceremony in his office in 1965, at which the Editors of *Time-Life* Books presented the White House with a leather-bound set of *Life*'s multi-volume *History of the United States,* he courteously received the gift but did not trouble to ask who the authors were, and he seemed to have no interest in opening any of the attractive volumes.

Johnson's interest in history appears to have developed as his own role in it expanded. The great men of his time had talked to him, making a reading knowledge of the subject superfluous. This conception of history was buttressed by his instinctive acceptance—as being sufficient for his needs—of the tutelage of Franklin D. Roosevelt and Sam Rayburn, the models who towered over all the other political figures he had known. Whenever Johnson talked of them he seemed to be indulging in a reverie in which he longed to find out how they, his adoptive fathers, might have wrestled with *his* problems.

Because men's vanities are tender, the estimations that historians make are rarely fully satisfactory to the subjects themselves. Yet, like portrait artists, historians must set down what they perceive; and when they are eye-witnesses their responsibility is exacting. They must be candid, yet not report more than they know or can defensibly infer. But they must understand from within as far as they can, not merely reflect surface appearances, however accurately. As professionals they have an office to perform that obligates them to serve posterity as well as to study the past.

I readily saw in Lyndon Johnson a novel kind of President: a well-groomed cowboy-figure in a handsomely tailored business suit. The clothes were the familiar badge of the imperious executive, but the cowboy style that went with the garb and was being sported in the highest reaches of government struck me as new. By cowboy style I mean what one learns early to associate with the species: a preference for action rather than the play of mind, a natural taciturnity, an inclination to divide people into "good guys" and "bad guys," and a practical understanding of the uses and dangers of firearms. The President's language, which was often ribald and scatological, also fitted the stereotype.

On the question of Vietnam, the President invariably sounded like a man who had studied methodically and hard the alternatives of policy open to him and, with a relentless searching of his mind and soul, had eliminated the less desirable. He had *decided,* in the literal meaning of the word, that is, by cutting off at last the anguish over his options and choosing the least unattractive. His manner always contained an element of hopefulness rather than optimism. He hoped, he was not sanguine, that the decisions he had taken would bring about a settlement in Vietnam politically acceptable at home. I believe I sensed in his words a certain weariness, stemming not alone from the exhausting business of consultation and reflection, but from the continuous fear that on the biggest decision of them all he might have been wrong.

By 1968 the clarity of his expectations, which had characterized his part of our conversations in 1965 and 1966, had given way to a bluer tone, less assured and more irritable. A querulousness about the men around him also gave a hint—however slight—of his vexation: their advice had not in fact shown him how he must untie the Gordian knot. I came to the conclusion the last time I saw him—although not on the basis of anything specific that he said—that he believed he had been led down a slippery path by men he had relied on too implicitly, and that he would willingly barter anything he owned or deserved for the chance of being able to retrace his steps.

16

President Johnson was unfailingly courteous and solicitous in responding to my questions, even though some of them, I know, irritated him and possibly heightened the suspicions he entertained of the academic community in general and of Eastern Seaboard intellectuals in particular. At some moments, our conversation became *his* monologue, as he apparently sought to make the most of the time he had set aside for our talk or to vent his spleen on a political opponent. Once, shortly after I stepped out of the Oval Office, Christian asked me casually whether the President had "rambled" and I had to say that I thought he had.

Our meetings—I could not but realize—were important to the President. Whenever he had to postpone or delay a scheduled session with me—a meeting of the National Security Council had run late, or a forthcoming State of the Union Message required intensive work, or it was necessary for him to be out of the country—he rescheduled it almost immediately. And a conversation never ended without my feeling that I had been able to ask him everything I could reasonably hope to ask about the subject at the time.

The friendly quality of the talks I had with the President's advisers undoubtedly reflected the President's own interest in the whole arrangement. Secretary of State Rusk was the most articulate of these men, being a hewer of powerful phrases, as well as a dogged advocate of the Administration's case for being in Vietnam. The fact that Rusk was not a lawyer seemed to give his arguments a zeal and sincerity they might not have had if he had been trained to "make a case." Rusk blended the subdued manner of a corporate administrator with the authoritative manner of an army officer. His humor was ready and warm—something I could not say of the President's—and the timbre of his voice lent grace to his expression.

Rusk was always prepared for my visits; he seemed to have thought beforehand about the possible contents of our conversations and budgeted sufficient time for them. Being a student of history, Rusk was interested in what I was doing. It always seemed to me that he spoke like a man constantly and vigorously seeking to apply the "lessons" he found in history to the issues he had been destined to face. His side of our conversations abounded in references to the historical precedents for halting aggression. It is no exaggeration to say that Rusk's confident knowledge of where he stood in the rushing stream of American history gave strength to his words and firmness to his acts. At the Tuesday lunch, Rusk always occupied the place at Johnson's right. He belonged there by right of protocol and also as the President's First Defender.

Secretary of Defense McNamara—who sat at the President's left at the lunches—was vigorous and businesslike in our conversations, eager to deal with the kind of questions I raised and ready to respond in philosophic language as well as in the language of a military chieftain. I do not think I only imagined that his administrative mastery of the Pentagon gave him rare self-assurance in talking about foreign policy and military possibilities. His crisp words and generalizations about the war in Vietnam blended with his long-range projections about the state of international politics in the next generation. The fact that his rimless eyeglasses gave him the look of an old-fashioned schoolmaster made him appear to be gazing harder at the world than most people, as if he were staring past the troubled present to the threatening future.

I was never sure when I had left the Pentagon whether I considered McNamara to be a "hawk" or something less aggressive—regardless of his public reputation, which varied from time to time. And I thought there was a marked ambivalence in his relationship to the President, even though I could not analyze its character satisfactorily. McNamara

18

was an intellectual who obviously did not have the intellectual's reputed fear of power; at the same time he appeared to me as a man of power who read more books than such men usually do, and consequently filled himself with ideas that sowed uncertainty in him as well as convictions.

McNamara and Rusk, being Cabinet officers, presided over huge bureaucratic establishments stretching around the world, and their own offices were, of course, in their Department buildings. Having burdensome duties not connected directly with the war, and being physically separated from the place where the decisions were made, were factors that always seemed to require careful consideration in judging their roles. To what extent were they responsive to their Departments and to what extent to the President? Were they more or less influential because they had to be called *to* the White House?

The White House, in the physical sense, was the place where the decisions were generated twenty-four hours a day. A visit to the basement of the West Wing quickly taught one how intense and incessant is the toil that precedes and surrounds decisions. In this unattractive set of offices much of the information that constitutes the raw data for making policy was received, sorted, sifted, and arranged for study and action. Directed by the President's Special Assistant for National Security Affairs, these rooms were the scene of preliminaries to foreign-policy-making that did not exist before President Eisenhower's time.

McGeorge Bundy was the energetic Special Assistant who served under Kennedy and for two years under Johnson; Bundy's successor was Walt W. Rostow. The position being new, it was not yet encrusted with tradition; moreover, being a Presidential rather than a Congressional creation, it operated legally as well as physically under the protection of the White House, and it still does. One was aware in approaching the Special Assistant's office that it was not yet haunted by its previous occupants gazing with cool appraisal from portraits on the walls.

Since Bundy and Rostow had both been professors in universities, they brought to their work the ease, informality, and opinionatedness that characterize successful academic people. Both men had been educated broadly in the social sciences and could sit in judgment on the political process they were seeing at first-hand, prepared to believe that the process would become amenable to an application of reason, tact, and force. Both men seemed deeply conscious that as students of power who had once enjoyed their scholarly detachment they were now on the inside pressing buttons themselves.

Bundy combined a personal reserve such as has long been regarded as typical of old New England families, of which his is one, with a familiarity that is the modern man's way of showing he is democratic and unceremonious. He and I and his older brother, William, the Assistant Secretary for Far Eastern Affairs from 1964 on, had been junior officers in the Signal Corps in the same army unit during the Second World War. This unit, based in Arlington, Virginia, serviced a predecessor of the National Security Agency, and the requirement of secrecy as well as functional separation had made our contact with each other only slight. Yet the fact of having been in the same outfit was an easy gambit in our conversation despite—or because of—the passage of more than twenty years. That Bundy had written on the making of foreign policy and had taught the subject as I, too, have for many years, also helped make our conversations seem comfortable and natural.

Rostow was better trained as a scholar than Bundy and his distinction as a man who had been "published" was widely recognized. Unlike Bundy, he had not been born to the patrician mantle, yet he and Bundy sounded astonishingly alike, their speech replete with striking phrases, analogies, and allusions. I remember thinking after I had talked with Rostow for a while, that his learned acquaintance with the jargon of academic political science when it was merged with the special language of Washington, took on a new and misleading aura of authority. Rostow, like Bundy, always spoke with an ever-present awareness that the man he worked for, the President of the United States, was upstairs in the same building. The physical nearness to the President and the fact of being *downstairs* no doubt were elements that became entwined in the making of decisions—creating a sense of being "in on everything" yet merely a servitor of the master.

The only other member of the Tuesday Cabinet situated in the White House was the Press Secretary. Bill Moyers affected policy for a time in 1965 to 1966 as profoundly as any other member of the Administration. His successor, George Christian, was far less influential, far less emotionally involved in national and international issues, and far less a confidant of the President.

Moyers was thirty-one years old when I first met him in 1965, the youngest man of power so close to a President since John Hay a century earlier had served as Lincoln's Assistant Secretary at the age of twenty-three. I received the instantaneous impression that Moyers combined better than anyone I had seen, the generalizing ability that characterizes the best men of mind, with the pragmatic vision that denotes the successful politician. Moyers' clean-cut words and gentle candor were disarming, not only as such but also because of his youth. He seemed to require no armor of mannerisms against the world and no subservience to help him deal with the President. When Moyers casually lit a cigar, he seemed to be not an old-fashioned politician but a modern one.

The first time that Moyers and I talked at length about

the War, I knew that his chief interest in my seeing the President and his aides was to help make known the President's ways of reaching decisions about Vietnam—an instructional task, incidentally, that the Tuesday Cabinet had not accomplished well, even though Rusk, McNamara, Bundy, and the President himself had once been teachers, and Moyers a minister. The second time Moyers and I talked, the Johnson Administration was significantly older and I recognized that my quest as an historian was no less interesting to him than the possible usefulness to the White House of anything I might have the opportunity of publishing immediately. Moyers had also become privately doubting of the war policies and was already exerting himself against any further expansion of the American military commitment in Vietnam. I know that he opposed as likely to be fruitless the bombing of the North Vietnamese oil and gasoline dumps, when that move was being deemed necessary by the "hawks" and escalatory by the "doves."

The professional voice of the "hawks" in the Tuesday Cabinet was General Wheeler, whose friends called him by his nickname, Bus. Wheeler struck me instantaneously as not a bookish man, but a man who read books. His life was shaped by ideas, though this did not show on the surface. Still, he was the first Chairman of the Joint Chiefs whose place resulted from his work as a staff man rather than from derring-do. In the era of the Cold War in which the threat of a nuclear war accompanied every outbreak, Wheeler turned himself into a thinker able to conceive of intercontinental hostilities and to think about the elements that would have to be engaged in order to conduct them successfully. This fact was reflected in his conversation, not in any belligerence or misanthropy, but in the ease with which he could link diplomatic and military considerations in international politics.

Wheeler and I held only one conversation. He was a

tense man—controlled in manner, yet forthright without being blunt. He had not long before been hospitalized for a heart attack. The experience probably helped bind him to the President, who years earlier had also suffered a coronary occlusion. Wheeler had a way of speaking about the President as if he meant "the Presidency"; the two were to him synonymous: he never mentioned the President by name. Whether this idiosyncracy told me something significant about his feelings toward the Commander-in-Chief or whether this was a reflection of the soldier's divorcement from the civilian leadership, I never could discover.

The Tuesday Cabinet was Lyndon Johnson's war-and-peace council. As such it met a need of the Presidency that was new in the nuclear age. It was a response to the requirement that the President be able to react to a crisis at any moment, on the instant, and with expertness—in short, that he be able to turn the White House into a command post. The old-fashioned full Cabinet meeting that consisted of the heads of the Departments is today only a memory as far as advising the President is concerned. General Eisenhower liked to discuss a wide range of questions with his entire Cabinet. But among modern Presidents he was, in this respect, an anachronism. The activist Chief Executives have never been able, or willing, to conduct their programs through this cumbersome instrument, more unwieldy than ever as it grows in size.

Although the President alone makes decisions, he depends on his advisers to give him directions (if not direction), warn him of pitfalls as he sorts out the alternatives, and give him encouragement when he has acted. Presidents lean hard on the men they trust. An unhappy consequence is that these men become highly publicized people, personages, indeed, few of them demonstrating the "passion for anonymity" that Franklin Roosevelt desired to see in the people around him. The advisers draw from their Chief the inspiration and prestige they require to be of help to him, and the more visible and powerful they grow the less useful they become. They find it harder and harder to say no to him, let alone break with him over policy when he and it are under attack. As time passes, an adviser's value to the President depreciates remarkably, but in the inner circle nobody notices the change because the personal ties have been annealed in the intense fires the President and his aides have endured together.

The Tuesday Cabinet probably was no exception to this rule. But in other ways, it was unique among the advisory groups that Presidents have assembled. It exerted the most influence on its leader. In the caliber of the men it contained and their power of persuasiveness it surely surpassed all others.

It was the first one formed to deal with foreign, not domestic, affairs; its members owed their places to their official position rather than to a special personal relationship with the President; all but one of the original members were holdovers from the previous Administration. Because of the weekly lunch date, as well as for other reasons, the Tuesday Cabinet became a formal institution.

Determinative as it was, it was also a mighty hammer for the Chief to wield, made more powerful as its members felt increasingly beleaguered and they turned toward one another for reassurance. If it is true that a President and his Cabinet are natural enemies, it may be said that the fateful work of the Tuesday Cabinet made its members his natural friends. Lincoln once wrote that he wished his closest advisers would "eat each other up and not their chief." Johnson never had to entertain such an idea. By temperament and training his men were not infighters, and they recognized fealty as the shining badge of gentlemen such as they. The President reinforced these tendencies in them by a royal presence and a paternal readiness to accept their political adversaries as his own, too.

The men of the Tuesday Cabinet wrestled tirelessly and continuously with a problem that remained essentially unchanging. The problem was tragically simple and painfully complex; at its core was an unprecedented conflict between American humaneness and American commitment. And in one of those overwhelming ironies of history, their nearness to the levers of military power rendered them impotent to resolve it. The report given in these pages of the way they thought, argued, and decided, may be a suggestive gloss on our times, as well as a representative fragment of the Johnson inheritance.

H.F.G.

Columbia University
December 2, 1969

I.

THE EVE OF MASSIVE ENGAGEMENT

IN THE EARLY WEEKS OF 1965 THE UNITED STATES MADE TWO major United States military decisions respecting Vietnam. One led to the first bombing of North Vietnam on February 7. The other resulted in increasing the United States troop commitment in Vietnam, beginning on April 10, when the first of 3,000 Marines landed at Danang air base. An increase in diplomatic activity matched these military developments. In an address at Johns Hopkins University in Baltimore on April 7 entitled "Peace Without Conquest," President Johnson offered to begin talks with North Vietnam without prior conditions, aimed at ending the war; he also offered to help create a vast development program for Southeast Asia. In the middle of May he authorized a six-day pause in the bombing designed to give North Vietnam an opportunity to consider entering into negotiations.

The American public was becoming aware in late May that the war in Vietnam was not going well. The South Vietnamese Army on its own was clearly unable to resist the forces it was called upon to face. The efforts to commence negotiations were stalled and the likelihood that the military involvement of the United States would continue to grow was becoming apparent. The force of American troops in Vietnam was expected to rise slowly to 60,000. For the first time, United States troops had been sent into battle, having hitherto been used only as "advisers" and as guards for the major air bases. On May 31 the troops of the Saigon government suffered what was described as their worst defeat of the year.

The shift for American forces from a purely defensive to a full role in the fighting in Vietnam was raising in the press and in journals of opinion the question of how heavily the United States was going to be engaged in war on the continent of Asia. The President was not unmindful of the implications of this public concern. He issued an appeal for fresh peace initiatives in a plea to the Soviet people direct. The well-informed reader of the press regarded the Soviet Union as a particularly important factor in ending the war. In April, Soviet Premier Aleksei Kosygin had associated himself with the Four Points of North Vietnam's Premier Pham Van Dong.* Secretary of State Dean Rusk issued a warning to the Soviets against bringing about a wider conflict through direct intervention in the fighting, alone or with the Chinese.

Meanwhile, the United States on April 28 had landed Marines in the Dominican Republic to protect American lives said to be endangered there. Two days later the President declared that it appeared "people trained outside the Dominican Republic are seeking to gain control." On May 2 the President identified the cause of the trouble as a "band of Communist conspirators." The forthright action taken in the Dominican Republic became linked with the war in Vietnam when the President requested of Congress on May 4 the sum of $700,000,000 in additional military appropriations for both undertakings.

During the first days of June the chief activities of Johnson that the White House reported consisted of reducing by 20,000 men the number of Marines ashore on the Dominican Republic, sending a special message to the Congress proposing to change the coinage system by reducing the silver content of the coins, traveling to Chicago to address the Cook County Democratic Party Dinner, greeting and conferring with Chancellor Ludwig Erhard of the West German Republic (who supported the United States in its Vietnam policy),

* See Appendix B.

delivering a commencement address at Howard University in Washington, D.C., in which he spoke of "the special nature of Negro poverty" and the role of the white community in causing it, and giving a commencement address at Catholic University in which he concluded: "Let us then open our doors and go forth together to work at each other's side toward peace. For let us never forget, the longest journey begins with a single step."

On June 9–11, 1965

THE EVERLASTING ISSUE OF PEACE—OR WAR—IS NO EASIER for a president to deal with today than it has been throughout most of American history, when electronic computers to supplement the mind were not even in men's dreams. No one knew this better than Lyndon Baines Johnson, who daily made resolute military and diplomatic decisions. In the second week of June, 1965, when mighty steps were being taken to enlarge the United States commitment of ground forces in South Vietnam, my opportunity to study President Johnson's method of making decisions began.

My first talk was with Secretary of Defense McNamara in the Pentagon Building, in his huge bright office commanding one of the best views of the city of Washington. His previous caller had been Ambassador Maxwell D. Taylor, home from his post in Saigon for the momentous discussions of policy.* He nodded to me absently on his way out. Taylor's presence there was a dramatic reminder to me—if any were needed—of how the nation's military and diplomatic activities had become intertwined, in Vietnam and elsewhere.

McNamara's greeting was gracious. He responded pleasantly to my recollection that we had met once before—on the wet afternoon three years earlier when Columbia Uni-

* A former Chairman of the Joint Chiefs of Staff, Taylor was Ambassador from 1964 to 1965.

versity awarded him an honorary degree. He took off his jacket, saying with mock seriousness: "It's gotten so I can't think with my coat on." He sat down at his huge desk, which had once been General Pershing's.

I had thought long and hard about my first question. In various forms I would put it again and again to the policy-makers in the next three days: "Mr. Secretary, when was the decision made to escalate the war in Vietnam?" I had made the question broad in order to permit the respondent to find his own "handle," as it were. At the same time by asking "when," I hoped to convey the desire that he should be precise.

McNamara dealt with the question head on. He said: "The steps were provoked, of course. The escalation has been going on gradually since 1954." He read to me from President Eisenhower's letter to President Ngo Dinh Diem* of South Vietnam, dated October 1, 1954,** which he "happened to have" on his desk. He instructed a secretary to make a photocopy of it for me. McNamara particularly called my attention to the sentence in which Eisenhower offered "to assist the Government of Vietnam in developing and maintaining a strong, viable state, capable of resisting attempted subversion or aggression through military means." McNamara emphasized that "escalation" by the United States, including the decision in 1961 to increase the number of army "advisers" in South Vietnam, was in answer to escalation on the part of North Vietnam, "an automatic response to North Vietnam's counterefforts to achieve its objectives."

He seemed unhappy with the word escalation as if it stood in the way of clarity and comprehension. The requirements for accomplishing the American mission, as Eisenhower defined it in that letter, had been rising, said McNamara, using

* Slain in a coup in 1962.
** The text is in *Public Papers of the Presidents of the United States: Dwight D. Eisenhower, 1954* (Washington, 1960), pp. 948–9.

military jargon readily; "the mission itself remains unchanged."

He went on to point out that when the United States met
the attack on its vessels in the Bay of Tonkin in August,
1964, with prompt retaliation against bases along the shore,
such attacks at sea ended. But, he added, "other escalatory
events" had not ceased.

VIETCONG TERRORISM

The methods of the Vietcong, he explained, were a key to understanding the character of the escalation by the other side.
The Vietcong marked for death or kidnapping village may-
ors, aldermen, school board members, and other local officials.
These tactics not only steadily drained the pool of natural
leaders in South Vietnam, but also created an atmosphere of
trepidation and physical insecurity. We could comprehend
what this meant to the public's morale, he said, when we
recognized that "the South Vietnamese have lost 1,600 local
officials in a population of 10 million"—the equivalent in
our own country, with a population 20 times as large, of
losing 32,000 significant officeholders. The South Vietnamese, he pointed out, had had 7,500 soldiers killed, proving that they were willing to fight against this abomination.

The attacks on Americans, beginning with the destruction
of military installations in late 1965, took advantage of the
fact that South Vietnam's political institutions have been
badly weakened. These attacks were saying to the South
Vietnamese, in effect: "See, not even the Americans can
protect themselves from the Vietcong." A result, McNamara
said without emotion, was to increase still further the anxiety and fear of the South Vietnamese people. I concluded
that McNamara regarded this campaign of intimidation as
the escalation by the other side to which the United States
was responding.

33

We discussed briefly the relative roles of Saigon and Washington in conducting the war. McNamara said that Saigon concentrated on combat while Washington concentrated on strategic objectives. Without my interrupting, he went on to talk about the role of the Joint Chiefs of Staff who used the principle, he said in an aside, smiling, that no members were more equal than other members. He mentioned the Cabinet, too, each member of which, he remarked, "has a directive from the President." Sensitive still to the failure of the Bay of Pigs in 1961, he said of his colleagues—military and civilian—that "over the years we have come to know each other better."

Our conversation turned next to the relationship between present policy and long-range military plans. Are we, I asked him, following a preset schedule of military steps in Vietnam? No, he replied, "military power is the tool of policy; the real future must constantly be compared with the forecasted future. When there is a divergence between the two, it is necessary to change either the objective or the means of getting there."

To help "get there," was the work of the Tuesday Cabinet, and I inquired about the form of these weekly meetings. McNamara explained that no decisions were reached at them. Their purpose was to "isolate problems" and to highlight for the President those calling for special attention. McNamara explained that the gatherings provided an occasion for the participants to say to one another: "Damn it, I think we ought to look into this." Decisions, McNamara seemed determined to have me hear, were arrived at in the Cabinet room. (I have not been able to find out what he meant.) There was modesty in the comment which followed: "You are always limited in your own understanding" of the situations you must handle.

As for his own conduct of affairs, he was pleased that his "cost-reduction program" had prevented a steep rise in the budget. As to his methods, he said he had a bias for action rather than inaction. "To take no action is to take undecided action," he declared. I believe he felt the import of this aphorism very deeply, that he guided himself by it and that even if he was quoting himself in uttering it, the words fitted the man perfectly.

I asked him what he thought about the scornful references in the quarters of the Administration's critics to "McNamara's War," reminding him of how the War of 1812 had long been remembered as "Mr. Madison's War." The designation did not cause him distress, he said, and he explained how the phrase had originated. In November, 1961, in a conversation with President Kennedy, he had "volunteered to look after" the war in Vietnam. In time, McNamara recalled for me, he made many journeys to Honolulu or Saigon for conferences and investigations on the scene. These trips identified him closely with the hostilities. He said he recognized no other significance in the sobriquet, and I did not pursue the matter.

We turned now to the war itself. Why were there no public heroes of the fighting? I asked—a question increasingly fascinating to me. He quickly responded that the war was being conducted from the Pentagon by the Joint Chiefs. He inferred that a "programmed war" cannot produce individuals who stand out, as previous wars had produced them. Still, he added, to be certain I understood what he was saying, the military was not running the State Department. Ambassador Taylor, being a general, perhaps created a wrong impression, the Secretary said, but there was no alternative to having him there. Was the Secretary satisfied with the American leadership in the field in South Vietnam? I asked. He replied that he was. I asked him whether he had been satisfied with the performance of Paul Harkins, the previous commanding general, who had served for four years. He "wasn't worth a damn so he was removed," he .

35

replied. "You need intelligent people." I did not ask why Harkins had been kept in the position so long.

Noticing behind the Secretary, in a collection of books, a copy of David Halberstam's recent critical examination of United States policies in Vietnam, *The Making of a Quagmire,** I asked him where he thought the United States had gone wrong in South Vietnam. I was thinking, of course, about the advice he might be called upon to give the President regarding the means of protecting the rest of Southeast Asia. McNamara replied that he thought it was too early to say if there were other things that could have been done in Vietnam. Did I have Thailand in mind? he asked me. Naturally I did. He answered that he had some ideas on the subject, but "it is a distractor" at the moment and that he did not want to discuss it.

We digressed from the war briefly when, in a lull, I asked him who his model as an administrator was. He talked enthusiastically and without hesitation of the Provost of the University of California at Berkeley when McNamara was a student there (1933 to 1937). The man was, he said, Monroe Deutsch, "the Jewish Greek scholar." From observing him, McNamara explained, he had learned that "there are few absolutes," and one must not see everything as black and white with "no gradations of gray." McNamara talked on about earlier days as his mind traveled to California for a moment. He had met Robert Oppenheimer, he said, and "Ken May* and his wife." As McNamara's mind swept toward the present again, he commented with a note of disappointment that in the 1950's there had been no "intellectual ferment" but "I am delighted to see the change in the 1960's."

The last question that I had time to ask McNamara—one

* New York, Random House, 1965.
* A well-known dissident member of the faculty.

I would put to others also—was: "Which historical analogy are you finding more instructive and compelling in dealing with Vietnam, the consequences of the appeasement at Munich or the consequences of the Chinese intervention in Korea?" He focused immediately on the Korean episode, asserting with confidence that drawing any analogy between it and the situation in Vietnam was "false in logic although significant in psychology." There would be "no sanctuaries this time," he said. As to a "land war"—involving the commitment of larger units than the United States had yet employed, and the engagement of North Vietnamese regulars or Chinese in uniform—he appreciated the dangers, he declared, but he brushed them off, saying "we are not moving in that direction."

A few minutes after leaving the Pentagon, I was at the Department of State—in the office of William P. Bundy, the Assistant Secretary of State for Far Eastern Affairs. We talked for a few minutes about our army days at the same post and then I began to put to him a line of questions similar to those I had put to McNamara. In response, Bundy, too, spoke of escalation as having been the result of a "succession of decisions" taken over a long period of time rather than of a sudden change of policy. And no one, he emphasized, "is happy about the present developments," which presumably was the decision, about to be made, to increase significantly the commitment of American troops in Vietnam.

PRESIDENTIAL POLITICS

I asked Bundy a question I had not asked McNamara and regretted I had not: Was the decision to bomb targets north of the 17th Parallel restrained until after the 1964 Presidential campaign was over? Bundy's answer was categorical: there was no relationship between the two events. Although

37

the White House had long recognized that bombing might be deemed necessary, he said, the President's resolve had been to keep looking for a better solution. If bombing had earlier seemed to be the only answer, he said, the President would have faced up to the need regardless of the political consequences. Bundy stated, however, without further explanation, that the attack on Bien Hoa on November 1— two days before the Presidential election*—"was not made the basis for retaliation."

Bundy himself headed the Administration's interdepartmental study-group to reexamine the whole problem of the war, in November of the previous year. Out of the study, he said, came the decision to make "a helluva try at stabilizing the political situation" in Vietnam—"a wise and right thing to do." Bundy, a lawyer, expressed himself in the language of his profession: the United States "couldn't outrun the client." By the beginning of December, a contingent decision had been made, he went on, that if the military situation did not improve, it might be necessary to bomb the North and to increase the United States' presence in Vietnam. But the steps agreed upon, he said, did not include either bombing Hanoi or using vast American ground forces. After the Vietcong attack on Pleiku in February, the United States had no alternative to implementing the earlier decision, except to permit a takeover of South Vietnam by Hanoi—or, at best, to stand aside and watch this end being accomplished in installments. Bundy said, however, that no one knows "how many [American] troops can go in without the deployment being misunderstood." A significant handicap, he said, was that it was "the white man" who was taking these steps. He felt confident there would be no outright commitment of division-size units. He was convinced, too, that China was reluctant to enter the fighting, and therefore

* A mortar assault that killed five Americans, destroyed five B-57 bombers, and damaged 22 others.

would not respond to the air attacks, adding that the North Vietnamese "don't want them in."

I then asked him a question that undoubtedly will interest future historians: Was there opposition within the Administration to "going north"? * I was referring to the widespread awareness in Washington that Undersecretary of State George W. Ball and Soviet specialist Llewellyn E. Thompson had argued for more restraint in United States military moves. Bundy responded with aplomb. "No one," he said sardonically, "was gay about this hotsy-totsy change in the war." Then he called attention to the concern, especially of "Tommy" Thompson—as he referred to him—over a possible Soviet response to American air attacks on North Vietnam. While Red China was not expected to react to these attacks, there was fear that the Soviet Union might take the opportunity to reassert itself as a friend of that part of the world. (After the Gulf of Tonkin episode in August, 1964, Bundy said, he surmised that Hanoi felt it needed "a better air-defense capability." But, he went on, Khrushchev was still in power and not until he was out the following month could Hanoi hope to fill its requirement through aid from the Soviets.)

I concluded that the opposition to the bombing was not a major element in the shaping of policy. But I could not be sure. The following day, when I returned to the Department of State to talk to Secretary Rusk, I asked him, too, about internal opposition. He was at pains to say that the advice to the President on the air attacks had been unanimous.

Rusk's welcome had been friendly and businesslike. When I said that the questions I wanted to ask were an historian's, not a newspaperman's, his face broke into a broad smile and he nodded.

In order to understand better how Rusk developed the

* Johnson's phrase, which he had used during the 1964 campaign, to describe a policy of bombing north of the 17th Parallel.

advice he gave the President, I asked him whom he considered his model among his predecessors as Secretary of State. Unhesitatingly, he named General George C. Marshall. Rusk said he had learned from Marshall—and "one cannot escape one's experience"—that a Secretary of State exists only to serve the President, who has "large, awesome, and frightful responsibilities." Regarding this relationship with the Chief Executive, Rusk affirmed, there could be no confusion. And "you don't resign," he added, "if the man who has to make decisions makes one."

Continuing his analysis, Rusk said that if the Secretary of State was going to discharge his duties properly, he had to keep a stream of ideas and suggestions constantly flowing to him from his principal subordinates. These people, he said with considerable feeling, are Presidential appointees who become "a burden if they turn into mere amanuenses. The key problem in a bureaucracy," he said pointedly, "is not power but the avoidance of responsibility." General Marshall, he said, had had a rule that every officer in the Department must steadily supply suggestions with respect to policies.

Rusk conducted his office with these precepts in mind. He relied heavily on his area chiefs—that is, on men like Bill Bundy. They were frequently on hand at conferences with the President, in order to help express the position of the Department of State on specific questions. Occasionally one heard it said that this style of presenting State's point of view weakened the position of State as against Defense, in that it tended to pit an Assistant Secretary against a Secretary, because McNamara did not speak through his subordinates. Rusk stoutly asserted, though, that better relations existed between his department and McNamara's "than I have ever seen or known in Washington before. There are contacts at all echelons." He pointed out as a further example that

40

officers of the State Department participated in the programs of all the War Colleges—the advanced-training centers of the armed forces.

I asked Rusk if he would compare the process of making decisions under Lyndon Johnson with the way it had gone under John F. Kennedy. I was surprised that he was willing to tackle this question. Johnson, he said, relies on "the statutory responsibilities of the Cabinet members." Kennedy, on the other hand, he said, had "an insatiable curiosity. He sought ideas from any source." Cabinet meetings under him were "seminar-type discussions." "People of no responsibility or rank might even be present," Rusk said. Johnson, he continued, had had "long and intimate public experience." He rephrased this point as he talked of Johnson's "long and responsible contact" with public problems: as majority leader, as Vice-President, and as a member of the Cabinet and the National Security Council. Johnson had served in Congress, Rusk said, and it was hard to find "a man better informed than a Congressman." Johnson sought a consensus in the country, Rusk went on. "He works for votes in Congress." He was "anxious to agonize over the other fellow's problems"—meaning the problems of Congressmen —even if he said no in the end. Kennedy, Rusk pointed out, came to office with only a slim majority and "he never knew where he was in Congress or in the country."

We turned to the war in Vietnam. Rusk responded with strong passion to some of the same questions I had asked McNamara and Bundy. The rate of escalation of the war, he said, had been determined by the other side. We had, he maintained, shown "patience and forbearance." We waited six months after the attack in the Gulf of Tonkin before commencing the regular bombing of the North (he did not mention the immediate retaliation, which, McNamara said, was why the attacks at sea had stopped), and we allowed four

41

years to pass after the North Vietnamese declared that they were going "to go after the South." *

Rusk said he thought it significant that the latest threat by the Vietcong against the South came after the 1964 election when "the incidence and character of the attacks changed." He said, "Perhaps the Communist world misunderstood our Presidential campaign." We declared we did not want a larger war, Rusk reflected, but they thought *they* could have one.

HANOI'S RESPONSES

The Secretary ticked off the various efforts of the Administration to seek a negotiated settlement, from "four years of bilateral discussions," through attempts to use the facilities of the Geneva Conference, down to the President's offer of unconditional discussions and the temporary suspension of the bombings.** In each case, Hanoi told the United States to "go to Hell." Now, Rusk said, he thought the Vietcong were going to see how well they could make out during the monsoon season that was about to begin in Vietnam.

"Dictatorship," the Secretary proceeded as we talked about America's general situation in the world, "underestimates democracy's willingness to do what it has to do." Since the Second World War, he said, a determined use of force had saved Iran, Greece, Berlin, Korea, the Philippines, and Malaysia—at a cost of 160,000 casualties. "NATO," he went on, "has put a trillion dollars into defense since 1947, 800 billion contributed by the United States." The underlying conflict, he said, "is between a U.N. kind of world and those trying to build a world revolution." The leaders of

* He was referring, I learned later by telephoning William Bundy, to the call upon its members in September, 1960, by the Communist party of North Vietnam in Hanoi "to liberate South Vietnam."
** See Appendix D.

"the other side," he declared, laid plans for Vietnam, the Dominican Republic, and the Congo. "Their declared doctrine of the world revolution," he insisted, "ought to be as credible as *Mein Kampf*." The consequences of not facing the problem of aggression were "enormous and dangerous," he said grimly.

I asked now: "Mr. Secretary, what kind of hearing do opposition ideas receive in the Administration?" Rusk replied without hesitation: "The Administration made no snap decisions." He continued, "No President has spent more time with his advisers than President Johnson." Even in the case of the Dominican Republic, Rusk said parenthetically, the President did not move hastily. The Ambassador of the United States crouched under his desk shielding himself from gunfire, Rusk explained, but nevertheless, the President held full discussions before he acted.

Rusk, like McNamara, dismissed talk of a land war pinning down American forces in Asia. "There are only 12,000 ground troops there," * he reported. "Does that look like a massive land war?" Of course, he added, there were 420 casualties last month and "no one fails to feel pain" over that fact. But, he concluded, the number of combat troops in South Vietnam only amounted to one-fifth of the number of American troops in Germany.

While on the subject of Europe, he seemed eager to point out that false hopes had been raised about a *détente* in the Cold War. Western Europe, he said, though it was prosperous, was militarily weak; it was still protected by 250,000 soldiers and "lots of megatons on the ground."

As we reflected upon the possible future course of events, he grew somewhat somber. He was pleased that 70 percent

---

* By the end of May, 1965, the Department of Defense records, 22,500 soldiers and 16,200 Marines were in South Vietnam. Rusk may have meant "troops in combat." (Mimeographed release "U.S. Military Personnel in South Viet Nam.")

of the public supported the government's position. "We are not under pressure here to get out," he said he had concluded. The public looks for good news, he went on, but "the future cannot be spelled out." Part of the difficulty in Vietnam, he pointed out, was that the issue of aggression was "not clear": the troops that were coming in were not coming in "in formation," as had been the case in Korea. He said with concern that there was "restlessness and anxiety" in the country and "we all have these feelings." The war would remain, though, he said, and we would have to "sweat it out." Vietnam was "mean and frustrating," he declared, as if to strengthen his observation; yet peace could be achieved in 48 hours if there were a willingness on the other side to have peace.

I looked forward now to going to the White House to talk to McGeorge Bundy in his office in the basement of the West Wing. I did not expect language from him different from that of McNamara or Rusk, both of whom had also once been professors. Still, I hoped to hear such special insights as might come from one who, as a scholar, had studied the diplomatic documents of other eras. Possibly he would be more consciously aware than his colleagues of how the insistent present becomes the historic past.

Early that morning, I had had an appointment with Bundy, but the very events I was looking for light on had forced an interruption of our discussion and a postponement of its completion until late in the afternoon. The reason for the change in schedule was a special meeting at the White House called by the President; Rusk (accompanied by Ball and William Bundy), McNamara, McGeorge Bundy, and General Taylor attended.

Bundy's manner as he prepared for that meeting had seemed relaxed. He had come out of his office to hand an agenda to a secretary for typing. As he did this he said to no one in particular, although smiling in my direction, knowing what I had come to discuss: "This morning, above all there will be orderly conduct of foreign affairs." The words had the ring of faculty-table humor.

Inside his office, our conversation had begun with some musings about the study of "decision-making." I ventured the idea that "decision-making" was a new "problem" in our affairs, invented by those who would make a science out of political analysis. Bundy, agreeing, spoke of how Dean Acheson had once looked his name up in the index of a book on the subject of "decision-making" in the Truman Administration, and had learned to his surprise that he had played the role of "a dependent variable." We laughed.

We had started to drink the coffee that Bundy's secretary poured for us when General Taylor, arriving for the meeting, stuck his head into the office. "I'll be right with you, Max," Bundy said. I broke off and rose to leave.

Eight hours later we began by discussing the place of Presidential advisers in our kind of political system. Bundy pictured them as prisms through which the President saw public problems. The President, he said, had to know how to read each of the prisms. Changing the figure of speech to the jargon of the tennis court, Bundy said that each man who advised the President had his own particular "spin" (he mentioned Chester Bowles, John McCone, and Adlai Stevenson), which the President had to allow for in receiving advice.

On the other hand, every adviser had to recognize that he was useful to his President only insofar as he attuned himself to the President's needs. Advisers have "got to do things his way. . . . When you work *near* the President," Bundy said, "you work *for* him. It is necessary to avoid a personal stake." Averell Harriman, he said, was very adept at attuning himself to the Presidents he had served.

How a President reaches a decision, Bundy believed was ultimately unfathomable, and had nothing to do with candor and openness. A President simply makes more decisions than there are ready explanations for. Bundy guessed that the reasons for the major decisions of President Eisenhower, "who was less a private man" than most recent Chief Executives, were probably fairly well understood by the men around him. Bundy said he thought that, in inscrutability, Franklin D. Roosevelt and President Johnson stood close comparison.

We then turned to the particular decision to bomb North Vietnam. It had been under discussion for about a year, Bundy said. "It was not easy to make." I came back to my question of the relationship beween the Presidential campaign and this decision. Bundy expressed his opinion that, of course, there had been political considerations to take into account. The President could naturally not help having these elements in mind. "President Johnson," he said, "is deeply concerned to follow the right road, but not split the country."

THE OPPOSING VIEWS

Once again I raised the question of opposition arguments. Were they being heard by the President? "The White House can argue with anybody," Bundy responded, confirming the belief that the contrary views were listened to intently. Bundy mentioned memorandums from Senators Mike Mansfield and J. W. Fulbright, which the President had read with care. Walter Lippmann, who was highly dubious of the Administration's policies in Vietnam, came in to talk with the President "regularly," Bundy remarked. As for contrary opinions within the Administration, Bundy said that he would not comment.

We touched next on the importance of the history of the fighting in Korea for the shaping of policy in Vietnam. "The lifeline politicians know," he said (presumably meaning Congressmen), that Korea "causes pain." But, he added, "Johnson is not terrified by Korea," though knowing that the issue "shakes the party."

I inquired about Washington's expectations from the bombing of the North. Bundy replied that Hanoi had reacted as anticipated. Even as it felt the "pain of the bombs," he said, it would continue to try to "dig apart and wear away the opposition of the South Vietnamese to the Vietcong." The bombing, he said, was chiefly important for maintaining South Vietnamese morale. And, he predicted, the decisive confrontation with the enemy would have to be in the South. "This fact makes the bombing irrelevant. There is nothing to bomb for. China would come in," he went on, "if we marched north of the parallel." Still, he added with confidence, "the Chinese want to stay out."

Because Johnson's hand in the military operations in Vietnam was so evident, even in the matter of selecting targets for air strikes, I asked Bundy about the usefulness of having the White House serve as a command post during crises. Bundy, who had seen President Kennedy use the White House in similar fashion during the Cuban missile episode, could reply with authority. "Who ran the Berlin airlift?" he asked rhetorically. Obviously, he went on, the battalions in the field cannot be directed from the White House. On the other hand, the country could no longer rely on the methods of yesterday, which were to declare war and then allow military events to take their course. The battlefields are an "arena of contest for political advantage." He recalled the now outworn simplicity of the instructions General Eisenhower had received in the Second World War; they went something like this: "Proceed to Europe and destroy the German armies." Bundy seemed to be saying that hereafter every President must conduct critical phases of his foreign relations as Johnson was then doing, making himself a more active Commander-in-Chief than was ever envisioned by those who wrote this Presidential role into the Constitution.

I went now to another question—one that only Bundy among the Administration's Big Four could answer. How did the conduct of American diplomatic affairs differ in reality from what it had seemed to be from the safety of Harvard Yard? Bundy thought that three things stood out. The first was the powerful influence of domestic politics in the formulation of foreign policies. He remarked especially on how essential it was to work in harmony with Congress in shaping policies. The second was the sensitivity of the press, although he added in an aside that the press was not as important as it thinks it is.

Above all though, Bundy felt, was the respect he had acquired for the role of the United States in the world, and for its influence on events when Americans make up their collective mind to do something with resoluteness and self-esteem. He remembered a visit to a Harvard seminar by John Foster Dulles when Dulles was Secretary of State. It was during one of the crises over Quemoy and Matsu, and the students as well as Professor Bundy were critical of the Administration's determination to prevent the seizure of the islands by Red China. Bundy said he now appreciated the import of what Dulles had said on that occasion, namely that, despite Harvard seminarians, he was not worried about the response of the American people.

I did not miss the analogy with Vietnam that Bundy appeared to be suggesting.

Bundy said he had come to accept also what he had learned from Dean Acheson—that, in the final analysis, the United States was the locomotive at the head of mankind, and the rest of the world the caboose—meaning, I thought, that he was not expressing chauvinism but simply passing judgment on the usefulness to the world of American energies.*

As I left Bundy's office, I glanced at the signed photograph hanging there of former Secretary of State—and War— Henry L. Stimson, whose autobiography Bundy had helped write. Stimson's stand against Japanese aggression in Manchuria in 1931 somehow seemed lively and relevant again— like Acheson's on the Berlin blockade and Dulles' on the offshore islands of China. I wondered whether Stimson's non-recognition policy had not in fact provided a valuable formula for avoiding Vietnams while seeming to take a strong stand against aggression.

I had expected to see President Johnson late the following morning but he ran behind his calendar and then held a meeting of the National Security Council at noon. While I waited for his schedule to open again, Bill Moyers invited me to have lunch in the White House messroom with him and his assistant, Hayes Redmon.

Moyers was the President's principal assistant. Almost every document that the President saw was seen by Moyers too. His answers to my questions seemed straightforward and ready, even allowing for the fact that he was a partisan.

At no point in the Vietnam crisis, said Moyers, did the President make a "peace or war" decision. The step-up of the fighting after the attack on Pleiku seemed only a promis-

---

* After the publication in *The New York Times* of the original account of this colloquy, Bundy maintained stoutly in telephone conversations with me that I had misunderstood his analogy. In a letter to *The New York Times* on July 5, 1965, Bundy wrote: "On this point Professor Graff honestly misunderstood me. What I said to him was that I have always strongly opposed any such view, and still do, but that since coming to Washington, I have learned to understand better the emphasis which Mr. Acheson and others correctly place on the importance of responsible energy in the conduct of American foreign policy."

ing option for ending the threat to South Vietnam. Moyers believed that the North Vietnamese misunderstood the meaning of the Congressional resolution in support of the President that was passed after the incident in the Gulf of Tonkin. They took it, he thought, as "a *pro forma* expression of American patriotism." (While he was speaking I recalled Dean Rusk's statement that Hanoi had not understood the meaning of the election campaign either. I could not fail to wonder if there were signals from the other side we also might have been misreading.) The current phase of the fighting—including stepped-up air strikes—Moyers said, was triggered by the attacks at Bien Hoa and Pleiku.

I asked Moyers my old question—whom was the President relying on most heavily for advice? He replied that the President was not "the prisoner of any man." Nor was he "the prisoner of statutory responsibility" (which I took to mean "the chain of command"). In addition to depending on the people I had had conversations with, the President talked to many other people in and out of Government service, including especially Dean Acheson and Abe Fortas, Moyers went on. Moreover, at the President's weekly breakfasts with Congressional leaders, more than half of the conversation invariably was about foreign affairs. President Johnson, said Moyers, "relies less on military advice than any President since Wilson." (I understood "military advice" to mean "advice from the military.")

Once again I pursued the subject of opposition within the Administration, and our conversation turned to George Ball. Moyers described Ball as a "necessary and effective devil's advocate, seeking diplomatic and political options which might be pursued." He "plays the role of seer, looking beyond many turns down the road. His avocation is to pursue a set of assumptions." And, Moyers said, Ball's words were heeded. Recently, Moyers recounted, some military advisers felt that the time had come to bomb closer to Hanoi than the bombers had yet ventured. Ball's arguments against this proposal, the President decided at the last minute, were determinative.

Furthermore, Johnson sometimes telephoned Llewellyn Thompson direct, in order to discuss Vietnam policies as they affected the Soviet Union. Direct phone calls flowed in the other direction, too. The Joint Chiefs, for example, could be in touch with the President without going through McNamara. Moreover, Moyers said, any President "would be a fool if he worshipped the system and thus denied himself sources except those at the top of the greasy pole."

In making decisions, according to Moyers, President Johnson consulted as widely as possible in the quest for alternatives. Said Moyers: "Ike's presence is very important," as if offering an illustration. In the Dominican crisis, Moyers continued, "he [the President] touched all the bases," and Moyers mentioned Milton Eisenhower, Abe Fortas, Luis Muñoz Marin, and Romulo Betancourt, as persons the President consulted. He discussed his speeches with Walter Lippmann. "The President is a skeptic about the advice he gets, but he takes it at face value and plays off one adviser against another." The President "has to be at the brink of action. He cannot refuse to take account of what may be logical."

Moyers described the President's skill in forcing his subordinates to look for a choice of possible solutions to the problems at hand—"options," Moyers called them. He was constantly probing, Moyers pointed out with evident satisfaction. (By actual count, Moyers said, the President had asked 41 questions at the meeting on Vietnam the day before—the one which had interrupted my talk with McGeorge Bundy.) It was obvious, said Moyers, "that the drama of working on the tip of a volcano affects him—and he is determined to avoid large-scale war."

Johnson devoured reports and memoranda with incredible dispatch, Moyers commented casually, but he was not a reader of books. Yet, Moyers hastened to add, he learned from history. The President was much guided by the American experience of the years 1938 to 1940. The President believed that the isolationist sentiment of that period greatly misled the Germans. Johnson much admired the way Franklin Roosevelt walked the line between lack of Congressional support and the necessity of providing moral and material help to the British people in 1940–41. Moyers concluded instructively that in President Johnson's eyes "Roosevelt is a book to be studied, restudied, and reread." The President often said "FDR was a second Daddy to me." Of course the press was an element in the making of decisions. The President knew he needed public support and that "a wind could drive it away." After a period at the beginning of his Presidency in which he "over-romanced" the press, he came to recognize that the press had immediate, not long-range, goals as he had. The President now concluded that "the First and Fourth Branches should be separated." While the President did not maintain that the United States had all the answers in the world, "the outcome [of events] is not beyond our influence." The President deeply believed that "no problems are insoluble."

Just as lunch was ending, word arrived that the meeting of the National Security Council had ended, and that the President would see me now. When I arrived at the Oval Office, he stood in the doorway reading a paper. Quickly finishing, he shook my hand and we went inside. He sat down in his rocker facing the fireplace wall, and motioned me to sit on the sofa next to the rocker.

The President knew what I had come to ask him about. I knew that he planned to be in Houston before the afternoon was over in order to greet the Gemini astronauts. I therefore went immediately to the point: "In the long history of fateful Presidential decisions we have scarcely any record taken contemporaneously from the Chief Executive himself as to what the process feels like. Mr. President, will you tell me?"

Mr. Johnson began to talk, one leg draped over the arm of his chair, a glass of root beer in his hand. He was somber as he said he had just left General Taylor, who was being separated by war from his wife for the third time in their lives. As the President contemplated what lay ahead, his thoughts lingered for a minute on what was past, for he said: "The worst mistake we ever made was getting rid of Diem."

WESTMORELAND'S REQUISITION

The President then pointed to a report on his desk—a statement from General Westmoreland of his recommendations regarding the forces he would require to succeed in his mission in Vietnam. The President said he would study it on the trip to Texas and over the weekend. He would consult with the Joint Chiefs of Staff, Taylor, the CIA, the Army, the Attorney-General, the Secretary of State, McGeorge Bundy, and Adlai Stevenson. He would have to decide by the Monday or Tuesday following. He said it would not be an easy decision; he proceeded to say why.

He talked in general terms of his choices in Vietnam. He had two, he said, both of them more provocative than present policy. There was the "Goldwater solution," which was the nuclear solution. On the other hand, we could pull out—which was really what Senator Morse* and Walter Lippmann wanted. Neither alternative being satisfactory, what were we to do? Should our forces just "hunker up and take it"? Clearly, no.

What was to be done? "What will be enough and not too much? . . . I know the other side is winning; so they do,

* Wayne L. Morse (Democrat, Oregon).

too," he said in a tone of realism. Then, more pensively, he added: "No man wants to trade when he's winning." In this case, we had "to apply the maximum deterrent till he sobers up and unloads his pistol."

It was not easy to send Americans to the jungles of Vietnam, the President continued. He wrestled with each decision night and day, he said, whether it was to bomb or to build up the strength of our combat troops. Only this morning, the President said, he had heard Mrs. Johnson being awakened by her maid. He called to the First Lady to find out why she was up so early. She replied that she had an appointment in connection with the beautification program. But why, she asked, was *he* awake so early? He answered that he was lying awake thinking of how he would feel "if my President told me that Lynda and Luci had to go to Pleiku in South Vietnam in a Marine company to do 'whatever was necessary to prevent aggression'—and possibly die." (He lingered a second longer than normal on "die," and, narrowing his eyes, he riveted them on mine.)

The President talked mournfully of the men who had been killed in action during the previous night—all with mothers, wives, sisters, friends. The toll in a larger war would be very much greater—"no one knows this better than I do." Still, Americans in Vietnam could not be "tucking tail and coming home. . . . It is my responsibility," he said, "to decide how to avoid that necessity." That was the business of the weekend.

Down at the ranch, he said, he wanted to think, "to smell some bluebonnets, watch the deer and antelope, and get some sand between my toes." He said softly that he was going to visit the graves of his parents and grandparents. (Later on he added he was also going to do some "hard praying.") He wanted "to roam by the river with nobody but a dog for company." In this setting he would try to decide. One guessed that the tension would then be over,

for he said solemnly: "I'm never bothered about a decision
I know is right." The process of deciding was patently under
way already, for the President was musing aloud: "When I
land troops they call me an interventionist, and if I do
nothing I'll be impeached."

When he mentioned interventionism, I turned the conversation for a minute to the landing of United States forces
in the Dominican Republic. "What happened there, Mr.
President?" The President was intense as he told me, pointing
to the kneehole of his desk a few yards from where we sat,
that the United States Ambassador was hiding in the kneehole of his desk trying to avoid being shot. "So I sent in
the Marines," the President said, measuring every syllable.
"And we took out 5,641 people from forty-six nations—
without even a sprained ankle. . . . Some of them were
Wilson's people, some of them Pearson's, some of them
De Gaulle's. Not even a sprained ankle," he repeated. "If
I hadn't acted, Castro would have had them all," he went on
angrily. "Now they call me an interventionist and they say
that I should have called the OAS. . . . Why," he said, his
voice rising slightly, "anybody smart enough to pour piss
out of a boot knows the OAS isn't going to send in any
Marines."

The President then talked with feeling and pride of his
34 years in Washington, which, he pointed out, began when
"Hitler was first rising to power," and of his long experience
in wrestling with diplomatic and military problems. He
talked of how President Roosevelt had wanted him on the
Naval Affairs Committee, because the United States had
"gotten rid of the Navy" and it had to be rebuilt. He
mentioned "the Nyes, the Borahs, the LaFollettes and
Chamberlain"—as if the whole panorama of the isolationist
years were to him like a remembered nightmare.

Asking for more root beer, which a messman quickly
brought, the President went on. He had battled to fortify

Guam and to arm the merchant ships. He had persuaded Cordell Hull * to write a letter in August, 1941, in support of the extension of the draft law; Speaker Rayburn had read it in the House just before the extension was passed by one vote. "I would like to think," said the President, "that my action in prompting that letter changed at least one vote. . . . Now they say that I am not qualified in foreign affairs like Jack Kennedy and those other experts. I guess I was just born in the wrong part of the country." He was dour as he added mention of his work on the Joint Committees on Atomic Energy and on the Armed Services Committee. He had gone through the Dien Bien Phu debacle and had been successively Minority and Majority Leader in the Senate, adding, "while Kennedy was on the Labor Committee." (The sarcasm was deep and biting.) The President went on: He knew that MacArthur had warned against a land war in Asia as long ago as 1941, yet SEATO had passed the Senate by 84 to 1. If the United States broke its commitment under that treaty, then "our word is no good." In bombing North Vietnam the United States was providing "maximum deterrence at minimum expense. . . . We are not provoking anybody but we will give them no sanctuary."

I am afraid I interrupted the President in order to go to another subject. On whom did he model himself, if on anybody, in the making of decisions? What had he learned from his predecessors in the White House?

He went first to the second question. Passing by Washington and Jefferson quickly, he said he liked Jackson's decisions, although he did not explain which ones. Then he skipped to Woodrow Wilson. "Did you ever meet him?" I asked. No, he replied, but his father had, and had talked about him at home. The President said that he admired Wilson's idealism. Like today, he added, we might have avoided a war if our intentions had been made clear. But, he reflected, "the Kaiser thought we wouldn't fight."

* Secretary of State, 1933–44.

The President left no doubt that Franklin Roosevelt was his model and prime example, which confirmed Moyers' observation. He remarked that Roosevelt's portrait hung on the wall across from his chair in the Cabinet room. He reminisced about the frequent Sunday lunches he said he had had with Roosevelt during the war years. A "perceptive man," and "reasonably deliberate," he called him, "who was determined once a decision was made."

Johnson had learned much from his German grandmother, too, he said. She had taught him caution: "Stop, look, and listen, and count to ten."

I brought up Lincoln's name. I had in mind Lincoln the war leader. But the President appeared to think only of Lincoln the emancipator. Lincoln, he said, "walks along the corridors with me; the Emancipation Proclamation is being made a fact." Returning to Franklin Roosevelt, he said with fresh firmness in his voice, "I share his social consciousness." To round out his reflections on the Commanders-in-Chief who preceded him, Johnson said he had worked with Eisenhower on the Lebanon, Suez, and Vietnam problems, and "tried to comfort" Kennedy after the Bay of Pigs when "he and Bobby thought they were right."

Having paid tribute to the past, the President turned again to the heaviness of his responsibilities. He drew from his pocket a piece of White House notepaper, which, judging from its appearance, had not just been put there. He read it aloud to me:

> Behind every enterprise stands the man who is ultimately responsible. The eager and able men on his staff spin golden dreams and propose new plans. They fret while he ponders. But to him, deliberation is sweet. He knows that success will have many shareholders, but that failure will be the sole property of the man responsible.

The President handed me the paper, telling me I could

57

send it back to him when I was finished with it.* He stood up, and as he did so he asked Marvin Watson, an assistant,** who had just entered the office, to obtain for me a copy of the statement "by the Roman general."

While we waited, the President said that the Philippines were sending 2,000 men to Vietnam and that South Korea was sending 2,000. Moreover, he said he had asked Prime Minister Wilson if he had any people he could send who had had experience with guerrilla warfare in Malaysia. As if to complete his account of his previous experience, he reminded me that he had won the Silver Star in the Second World War for helping shoot down "20 Zeroes."

Watson soon re-appeared, bringing me copies of three documents which were in frames on the wall above the President's desk in the small auxiliary office adjoining the Oval Office, where, Mr. Johnson said, he worked late at night. One was a portion of a speech by a Roman consul of the second century, B.C., headed: "A Roman General's Opinion of 'Military Critics.'" Another contained words by Edmund Burke on the subject of the thick skin required by public men. The third was a quotation from Lincoln in the same vein.

The President took me into the auxiliary office—which he called "my little office." I had the feeling that he wanted to show me where he made some of his decisions. He spoke again of his family—of his wife and mother and father. Before his mother died, he had always consulted her on his important decisions. As he talked we stood almost nose to nose. Politely, the President asked me if I had any further questions. I felt I should not keep him longer, and we said good-bye.

* Afterward I learned that the words came from a page of a desk calendar passed along to him by a member of his staff.
** He was Postmaster-General in the last months of the Administration.

From this series of conversations, a few things seemed certain. The men around the President did not speak of conquest on the battlefield in Vietnam—as men from time immemorial had talked of victory. Being honest men they knew that there could be none. Yet, they were filled with the resolve of people who did not mean to accept defeat either. Beyond the specific advice they were offering the President daily, they buttressed (one may surmise) his own resolution to see this terrible episode through to a satisfactory end. They were alive to the fact that they, too, were accountable to history.

As for the President, he left the unmistakable impression that he was his own man, his own "decider." The day before I was in his office, McNamara had informed him of General Wheeler's views on the Westmoreland requisition. Wheeler being out of town, Johnson said he would wait until Wheeler returned in order to hear the General's opinions at first hand.

Amid the turmoil involved in making big decisions the President seemed to keep his balance and maintain an attentiveness to detail. The night of the attack on Pleiku, for example, Rusk, who was in Florida, called George Ball "collect" at the White House where he was in conference with the President. Said the President, as the call interrupted them: "George will take it and charge it to the State Department, not the White House."

Johnson was also a man of peace, despite the two-gun impression of him the world had recently gained. Moyers said that the President was "less a hawk than any man in this government." ("God knows peace would be so sweet to us," Johnson had said at one point in our conversation.) It seemed ludicrous to call him, as one critic did, "the gendarme of the world counterrevolution." Moreover, despite his earthy language and regional drawl, which he would have been the first to say were handicaps in the traditional conduct of diplomacy—if not of war—he knew there was a world beyond the Pedernales, or even the Potomac, with which he would have to come to terms. This may have been a neglected but essential point in distinguishing him from Goldwater and his followers. And Johnson's long experience on the Hill, far from being a handicap, was a distinct advantage: it had taught him to look at a proposal from the other person's point of view—as well as his own—even when he eventually would have to oppose it.

Johnson's effusiveness sometimes appeared out of date and lacking in subtlety—a handicap in establishing a relationship with young men and women that he was well aware of. His apparent need to embrace people by seeming to take them into his confidence may, in fact, have been a substitute for the people's affection, which Johnson craved and which eluded him. Still, he was as determined as Franklin Roosevelt, who so fascinated him, might have been, to be unflinching in the face of the grievous long-standing problems it was his destiny to fall foul of.

In the President's private quarters in the White House hung a photograph of Roosevelt talking to Johnson, taken about thirty years before. The typed caption on the mat, Johnson's own, read: "I listen." These were remarkably fitting words to describe Johnson's stance at that moment, as a maker of foreign policy. He sat with one ear cocked for whatever counsel he could hear, for whatever increase he could produce in the number of alternatives available to him, and with the other ear he strained to hear a sound, however faint, from Peking or Hanoi, that the hour had arrived at last to sit down and talk.

Between March 31 and June 30 the number of American military personnel in Vietnam had doubled, bringing the total to 59,900. As June progressed, a new stage in the fighting was beginning: American men were about to be sent in units into open combat, rather than only guarding bases and carrying on patrol duty. Nevertheless, the troops were not to be used to initiate offensive action against the Vietcong; furthermore, the air strikes on North Vietnam were being confined strictly to non-industrial targets some distance removed from Hanoi and Haiphong.

Although the Administration gave assurances that it was following a policy of exerting only limited pressure on "the other side," Secretary McNamara announced on June 16 that 21,000 more Americans would be sent to South Vietnam. He declared, "We will do whatever is necessary to achieve our objective." The President had the powerful support of the Chairman of the Senate Foreign Relations Committee, J. William Fulbright of Arkansas. Fulbright answered critics of the Administration who said that the United States had no business involving itself in what was essentially a civil war in Vietnam: ". . . unconditional American withdrawal . . . would betray our obligation to people we have promised to defend . . . would weaken or destroy the credibility of American guarantees to other countries and . . . would encourage the view in Peking and elsewhere that guerrilla wars supported from the outside are a relatively safe and inexpensive way of expanding Communist power."

In July the situation in Vietnam worsened politically— the government of General Nguyen Khanh seemed on its way out—and the Vietcong were pressing the attack. The President sent Henry Cabot Lodge, who had served as Ambassador in Saigon in 1963–64, back for another tour of duty. On July 28 President Johnson announced that 50,000 more Americans would be sent to Vietnam, and "additional forces will be sent as requested." The burden of the ground war was about to be taken over by the United States. Amid these developments, Justice Arthur J. Goldberg was persuaded to leave the Supreme Court in order to become the United

States Ambassador to the United Nations, succeeding Adlai E. Stevenson who was suddenly stricken.

Steadily the Administration probed for peace, seeking ways to begin scaling down the war. Still, peace seemed far away. By October the number of American troops in Vietnam was expected to rise toward 200,000 before the end of the year. Most observers believed that the Vietcong had been badly hurt and that a "real" rural pacification program could soon be commenced. At the same time, the opposition to the Administration's policies was growing, especially on the campuses of the country. A variety of street demonstrations, teach-in and sit-in rallies and marches were mobilizing young people almost everywhere. One form of positive action some Americans were taking was an attempt to undermine the military draft. Their argument was that the war, especially the bombing of North Vietnam, was immoral and unconstitutional. Yet the apparent successes in the field against the Vietcong were helping to raise the percentage of people who declared themselves in favor of the Administration's policies. Former Vice-President Richard M. Nixon predicted that Vietnam would become a major issue in the mid-term elections of 1966 unless the Johnson Administration laid plans "to win the war . . . and to end it."

Even those who were encouraged by the military reports from Vietnam, however, were unable to define what "victory" might be like. Unless pacification succeeded, it appeared, the military effort would have been in vain. In addition, the increasing ferocity of the fighting—a result not only of United States troop increases but also of North Vietnamese infiltration of troops via the Ho Chi Minh Trail —led to a growing unease in Washington and elsewhere that war between the United States and Communist China might be the outcome. As the year 1965 drew to a close, the possibility of a negotiated peace continued to appear very slim.

II.

THE CHRISTMAS
INITIATIVE FOR PEACE

BY CHRISTMAS 1965 THERE WERE ALMOST 185,000 AMERICAN soldiers, sailors, and airmen in Vietnam, and the end of the escalation was not in sight. The United States, moreover, declared that it felt free to undertake military action in Cambodia if necessary in order to protect American troops in South Vietnam. Already the bombing of the Laotian infiltration routes was being intensified and decisions had been taken to build more airfields in Thailand. On the diplomatic front there was no apparent progress: in plain fact, each side was telling the other to get out of South Vietnam.

Still, the Administration seemed determined to try to move the war to the negotiating stage. On December 23, it opened what was widely heralded as "the Johnson peace offensive." This step consisted of halting the bombing of North Vietnam and dispatching a number of American diplomats to various capitals in order to explain the United States' position. Secretary Rusk met in Saigon with South Vietnamese officials and Vice-President Hubert Humphrey met with Soviet Premier Aleksei Kosygin in New Delhi; Ambassador to the United Nations Arthur Goldberg visited Pope Paul VI in the Vatican. The diplomatic initiative included also an appeal from Goldberg to Secretary General U Thant restating the desire of the United States to withdraw from South Vietnam as soon as that country was strong enough to stand on its own. Goldberg reiterated President Johnson's offer to commence "unconditional negotiations."

Hanoi's response to this worldwide effort was negative. The President, in the face of his disappointment, told Congress in his State of the Union Message in January, 1966: "Our decision to stand firm has been matched by our desire for peace." An increase in the number of United States men in Vietnam was now expected as the Administration prepared for the worst. As the month neared its end, the President was under heavy pressure to extend the bombing pause. Senator Fulbright, who had begun to shift his position so that he was now increasingly critical of the Administration's war policies, declared that a resumption of the bombing would thwart any chance of getting negotiations started. He feared, he said, that there would be an "ever-increasing escalation in the fighting." On the other hand, the President was concerned about the military advantage that the bombing pause was producing for North Vietnam. Distressed and personally torn, on January 31 he ordered the bombing of the North resumed—ending a truce of 37 days.

President Johnson emplaned for Honolulu on February 5 in order to confer with the South Vietnamese Premier, Nguyen Cao Ky, and with the United States civilian and military leaders who also flew there from Saigon. The President's chief aim was to help strengthen the South Vietnamese government which, although still far from vigorous, had nevertheless lasted in office eight months. Recognizing the need for the South Vietnamese government to develop its influence on the countryside, the United States was determined to place new emphasis on the rural "pacification" program. Still, the military requirement was easiest to satisfy at the moment and in Washington there was talk of raising the number of American soldiers in Vietnam to a half million. In the third week of February, the Senate Foreign Relations Committee held intensive hearings on the war as millions watched and listened on television. The Committee, in effect, was challenging the Administration to defend the American prosecution of the war: the purpose, the strategy, the likely outcome, and the cost.

The Administration defended itself principally through Secretary Rusk and General Taylor. Taylor described the war assuringly as a limited one, "limited as to objective, as to geographical scope, as to weapons and forces employed, and as to targets attacked." The most caustic of the critics was Senator Morse, who boldly and angrily predicted that the American people "will repudiate our war in Southeast Asia." Senator Russell B. Long of Louisiana, the Democratic whip, maintained that public criticism of the Administration's position "will do nothing but encourage the Communists to prolong the war."

In the matter of military strategy the Administration was defending the policy of "search and destroy" as best calculated to keep pressure on the enemy. Critics were declaring this strategy wasteful of lives, likely to lead to all-out war, and incapable of bringing the war to a successful conclusion. They argued instead for an "enclave" strategy, under which the allies would confine themselves to maintaining relatively small and easily-defended positions. These would be held until such time as the Communists were ready to negotiate a settlement.

Plainly a significant issue was whether or not the National Liberation Front (NLF), the political arm of the Vietcong, was to be allowed participation in the responsibility for governing South Vietnam. Senator Robert F. Kennedy caused a considerable stir when he declared himself in favor of such an arrangement. The Administration's response was quick: Vice-President Humphrey asserted that permitting the Vietcong in a South Vietnamese government would be like putting "a fox in a chicken coop."

On February 22–23, 1966

HOWEVER FUTURE HISTORIANS WRITE ABOUT VIETNAM, contemporaries knew that the war had entered a new phase in the beginning of 1966. The fulfillment of the promises made at Honolulu by President Johnson depended not only on the national treasury but even more heavily on military success in the field. And after the peace offensive had failed, a military solution in Vietnam seemed easier to reach than a diplomatic one. Plans were being made in conformity with this fact. The plans, as always, reflected the temper, the mood, and the assumptions of the President and his principal consultants.

In the third week of February, I had a fresh opportunity to assay these elements in conversations with the President and his aides. I had talked to most of the same men in June. This time, in addition to President Johnson, Secretaries Rusk and McNamara and Messrs. Moyers and Bundy, I talked to Under Secretary of State George W. Ball, Assistant Secretary of State for African Affairs G. Mennen Williams, and Moyers' deputy, Hayes Redmon.

The round of conversations began early on the morning of Washington's Birthday. It was a brisk, clear day and the public buildings were almost deserted. The flags were at half-staff in mourning for Admiral of the Fleet Chester W. Nimitz. I remember thinking as I walked toward the Department of State from my hotel that the city of Washington wore an air of melancholy appropriate to the subject I had come to discuss.

I called first on George Ball, a tall, hulking man whose manner was that of no nonsense. A lawyer by profession, he had been in and out of government service for thirty years. I wanted especially to talk to him because in the aviary of Vietnam policy-makers he was labeled a "dove."

Moreover, as Counsel to the French Embassy in Washington during France's war in Indo-China, he qualified as a student of Vietnam affairs longer than anybody else in the Administration.

My first question was, as usual, direct: "Mr. Ball, tell me what lay behind the peace initiative of last January?" Ball's answer was equally direct. "We were," he said, "seeking to get a process started." It was an effort to "break the deadlock"—"there was no sign of movement at Hanoi." Several East European countries "had indicated that their efforts at seeking to end the war were foreclosed by the air offensive against the North." This notion, he said, had been implied by the Soviet Union, too, "but mostly by the East Europeans." The neutrals and our allies had also been making such an argument, he said.

THE BOMBING

I asked Ball if the cessation of the air attacks on the North had taken place with an eye on the possible favorable political effect it could have in some places here at home. Ball replied that politics can never be excluded, "nor should you or could you." The bombing halt, he went on, had been discussed "at the Ranch" when Rusk, McNamara, and Bundy were there. "Troop deployments [by the enemy] were increasing," and it seemed right to try to "interrupt them." Still, the holiday season had advantages, he pointed out, because Christmas and the Vietnamese festival of Tet coincided on the calendar. The "general stand-down over Christmas" set things in motion, he said.

We turned to the matter of the resumption of the bombing, which had followed the brief "stand-down." Was there, I asked, opposition within the Administration to the resumption? I was only half-prepared for his answer as he shot back sharply—but neither apologetically nor defiantly: "I was the opposition."

In continuing to talk, he gave me what he described as "the balance of elements" for and against the resumption. There were, he said with impressive precision, four arguments in favor of resumption and he listed them. First, it was necessary in order to maintain the morale of the South Vietnam government and people and of our own troops by denying the enemy immunity from the cost of aggression. Second, it was necessary in order to interdict partially the movement of military goods from the North to the South— "to make the flow of supplies more costly to North Vietnam." Third, it was necessary in order to convince North Vietnam finally that the war would not be worth the price, that there was "a danger of the ultimate destruction of the economic life of the country." It could be anticipated, he said, that this factor would "operate on the decision-makers of the regime in Hanoi." Fourth, it was necessary because a failure to resume the bombing would be taken by the world as a sign of weakness. If we yielded to world opinion in this matter of continuing the bombing halt, Ball said, we would be expected similarly to yield on other matters as well.

Ball then took up, in the same even voice, the arguments against resumption. First, he said, since the increased American presence in Vietnam—which began in February, 1965— the fear for the morale of South Vietnam had ceased to be a serious concern. Second, the use of bombing to interdict the shipment of supplies could make these supplies more costly, but the bombing could bring about no "political consequences," because the enemy forces "have small requirements" and "live on the country. . . . Five hundred pounds can be transported by a coolie on a bicycle." Ball then observed: "Giap* has come to the same conclusion. . . . One thing the Orient has is manpower."

* General Vo Nguyen Giap, North Vietnam's Minister of Defense, Deputy Premier, and hero of Dien Bien Phu.

Ball went on: A question to be asked is whether military pressure like bombing "can be translated into a political decision." One effect in "a doctrinaire police state," he pointed out, could be "to dig people in further." He had learned much, he said, in his role as a director of the United States Strategic Bombing Survey at the end of the Second World War, which had systematically studied the effects of the air attacks on the Axis countries. Moreover, he said, having once been a legal adviser to the French government, he was "well aware of the French experience in Indo-China."

The third point bore, he said, on the danger of involvement with China. There were, Ball observed, two wars in Vietnam, one in the North and one in the South. China could be expected to respond one way when a "war of national liberation" was at stake, as in the South, and another way when "direct military damage was being inflicted on a sister Communist republic," as could be said to be the case in the North. Moreover, he said, air attacks on the North might bring about a progressive loss of the power of decision in Hanoi. He explained: Hanoi might become "less free to make decisions without reference to Peking." Thus, he summarized, a resumption of the bombing could, in effect, prove to be an "impediment to peace."

When the points on both sides were carefully weighed, he thought, the controlling one related to the interdiction of men and supplies. He described that argument as "very impressive." Once the decision to send troops into South Vietnam had been made, he said firmly, it became necessary "to do everything possible to minimize our losses"—even if the relief was only marginal. Ball concluded this part of our conversation by saying that President Johnson had designated him to write the brief opposing resumption. Bill Moyers later told me that this document of eighteen pages, and of "rare brilliance and lucidity," reached the President one midnight and that he read and weighed it immediately for three hours.

We then went to a subject that was also of major concern to me. What, I asked, is the position of Red China in this whole matter? Ball's answer showed that he was a man who had lived with the question and its corollaries for a long time. He was sure, he said, that the presence of the Americans in the Vietnam conflict increased the pressure on China because it affected the competition between Red China and the Soviet Union within the Communist world.

"China," Ball went on, "probably doubts whether we ever intend to get out of Vietnam. They see our installation at Cam Ranh Bay, which represents an investment of $100,000,000, and it looks permanent to them." He added sternly: "They just don't know how anxious we are to get out of that stinking country." The Chinese, he continued, hope the United States will regard itself as "stuck in a glue pot, and will tire and quit." While waiting, the Chinese will fight "to the last Vietnamese."

We talked about the significance of sparing the harbor of Haiphong from American bombing attacks. "Haiphong," Ball said, "is the lifeline of North Vietnam to the Soviet Union. If the United States were to change its present policy and deny the use of the harbor to Hanoi," he said, "the effect might well be to bestir the Soviet Union." He said he believed that such a step taken by the United States might force the Soviets either to abandon North Vietnam, or, in order to continue to supply it, to deal with Peking. Furthermore, he added portentously, the issue had to be raised as to whether the Soviet Union "would ever stand down twice from a blockade"—the first time, of course, had been during the Cuban missile crisis in 1962.

At this point I asked Ball to do some predicting: "What is your informed guess as to how things will go from now on?" One outcome to be looked for, he said, was a disintegration or unraveling of the hostile forces in the South. Hanoi, he felt certain, would decide what to do, after the Vietcong fell apart. They would not call off the Vietcong first. He gave it as his opinion that the Vietcong were now finding it harder and harder to retrain and regroup. They were losing their sanctuaries and had to keep moving, a situation he called a "demoralizing and debilitating experience." "There is a growing conviction," he said, "that the Vietcong are not going to win." Desertions from their ranks were taking place "singly and as units," he reported.

The war would not end on a single day, Ball was sure. It would probably end, he thought, "with a whimper, not a bang." Peking, Ball believed, could accept the defeat of the Vietcong—unless the war took a new course which made it necessary for the United States to "take out" MIG bases on Chinese territory. However, he added quickly, "I think you can do a helluva lot in the South with relative impunity."

I asked him what effect his negative view of the bombing of the North was having on his relations with Rusk, who was regarded as a "hawk" in the public press. Ball seemed mildly amused that I should ask this question and he said: "As far as we are concerned today, we haven't got any options. . . . I am greatly concerned over the hand-wringing I see. . . . The one thing we have to do is to win this damned war," he said resolutely. Until the previous July, when the commitment of troops was vastly increased, he said in an afterthought, it had been possible to make "a different decision." But he added thoughtfully, "there is no longer any useful argument to be made about current policies."

Switching to another theme, I asked him a question which I was planning to put to the other policymakers as well: What has happened in America to create among so many former internationalists a growing reluctance to be involved in the kind of burdens the struggle in Vietnam imposes? Ball responded confidently, beginning with an observation that the phenomenon I was talking about was a product of the post-Stalin world. Many people, he said, had come to the conclusion that Communist power has become "more benign" and that "the dangers are not as great."

Just as Ball was about to amplify his remarks, his phone rang with urgent word that he was wanted at the White House for a meeting. (I found out afterwards that the subject to be discussed was Senator Robert Kennedy's proposal for the United States to promise to bring the Vietcong into the Saigon government—a suggestion that had produced a brouhaha in the press the day before.) As Ball prepared to leave, he proposed that we continue our discussion later in the day. Unfortunately, this was not possible.

A few minutes later I was in the office of G. Mennen Williams, on the floor below Ball's. Williams, a former governor of Michigan, who had just completed five years as Assistant Secretary in charge of African Affairs, had played a large role in the peace offensive. In a period of seven days, he had visited fourteen African countries. The news that a peace offensive was being undertaken had reached him unexpectedly, he said. It was noon in Detroit on the last day of the year, and he had just gotten out of the dentist's chair when he received word to hurry back to Washington. By four or five o'clock, he was in his office. After being briefed by Rusk, William Bundy, and U. Alexis Johnson, the Under Secretary of State for Political Affairs, he was on his way to Africa.

"What precisely was your mission on this unusual journey?" I asked. Williams replied that he was to explain the American position to "the other side" through the agency of the African nations. In brief, he said, we hoped to "commence a dialogue." I asked him why he had had to visit so many countries. Did we not know where the good contacts were? He explained simply, "If you talk to one country you have to talk to another." Another aim, he said, in an apparent afterthought, was to put on a demonstration to the African nations that the President of the United States regarded them as important.

REACTIONS IN AFRICA

What, I asked, were the results of your efforts insofar as you could judge them? "All the leaders to whom I spoke reacted most warmly and favorably to the fact that the President of the United States had sought them out." Williams said he thought that their response provided convincing evidence of how successful the United States diplomacy in Africa had been during the previous five years. The Africans, Williams went on, appreciated the President's suspension of the bombing. Moreover, they were unanimous that the President's Fourteen Points* were "a reasonable, viable basis for peace."

I interjected that, of course, the African leaders already knew of the President's points because they had been so widely disseminated. Williams' answer somewhat surprised me. He said that Julius Nyerere of Tanzania had remarked to him, "I did not know that you accept the Geneva Accord." Prime Minister Milton Obote of Uganda, Williams said, had also expressed astonishment at the fact. (Williams said, however, that the United States Ambassador in Uganda confided to him, after the conversation with Obote and his people, "Hell, we had told them this.")

Williams said that the Africans were unanimous in saying of point three in Hanoi's proposals:** "Of course you can't accept this." In Algeria, he said, Premier Houari Boumedienne and his foreign minister interrogated him closely on point thirteen of the Administration's proposal,† and Williams gave them assurances that the Vietcong would be heard, that representation for the Vietcong would "present no problem."

Why, I asked, should the Africans be interested in helping

* See Appendix C.
** See Appendix B.
† See Appendix D.

to bring the Vietnam war to a close? First of all, Williams replied, "Africans do not like war; they like to see things settled by discussion." Secondly, most of them regarded the war as having the effect of reducing aid to them in the long run. And, thirdly, "they are not all so fond of the Chinese." Over and over, he remarked, he heard leaders say "be careful of the Chinese." The African leaders also regarded the war in Vietnam as "Chinese imperialism," Williams said. He had heard this opinion especially in Morocco, Tunisia, Liberia, Nigeria, and Senegal. The leaders said "be sure your heads are screwed on" so that "you are not taken by the Chinese."

"Which countries," I inquired, "seemed active in trying to further the purposes of the peace offensive?" He listed for me Algeria, Mali, Guinea, Ghana, Uganda, and Kenya. Morocco said it had no contacts. "Nyerere could have done more but he didn't. . . . We're not pushing them," he said resignedly.

I asked Williams if there had been any follow-up on his visit to Africa. Yes, he said, he had the African ambassadors brought in for talks "after this Hawaiian thing"—referring to the President's journey to Honolulu to meet with Premier Ky. What worries the Africans most, he lamented, was the statement by Premier Ky that South Vietnam would not deal with Hanoi and the Vietcong. That unfortunate statement, Williams remarked with irritation, had been dragged out of Ky by television men and newspapermen who had "backed him into a corner."

Williams summed up his role in the peace effort: "I was gratified that I might have a part." He had had no illusions about the outcome, he confessed. "There was no reason to believe that the Africans would succeed where others had failed. There was simply the hope that the weight of the non-aligned countries might be more impressive." He also said he thought the effort "helps Goldberg at the UN, who chats with the ambassadors from time to time."

"The Africans," Williams declared, "don't like war." And

again: "Most of them feared that any expansion of the war would hurt aid to *them*."

We stopped our conversation only because I had an appointment with Secretary Rusk. But as I stepped outside Williams' private office, his secretary said Rusk had left word for me that he could not keep our date. He had been called away—to the same meeting that Ball had rushed off to attend. I telephoned Rusk's office and we moved the hour for the planned conversation to late afternoon.

After lunch I headed toward the Pentagon to see Secretary McNamara. I arrived a few minutes early so I walked to the end of the mall in front of the River Entrance to the building. From there one can see almost all the postcard landmarks of Washington, a heady setting in which to consider what one asks the Secretary of Defense in the midst of a war. I had a feeling I cannot explain that he might answer me more fully than any of the others—if only I could find the formula for producing this result. As I sat in his outer office a few minutes later, I stared at an example of military art on the wall, a painting done in 1962 entitled "U.S.S. *Thomas Jefferson* Amid Icebergs."

McNamara made me feel welcome and I sat down in the armchair next to his huge desk. I had decided to put to him as my first question the one which was coming more and more to fascinate me, the one Ball had not been able to finish answering: What has happened in the country to make the internationalism of a few years ago seem less and less attractive to so many thoughtful Americans?

In his characteristically confident language, McNamara went straight to his answer. "You mean neo-isolation," he said slowly; and then more crisply, "I should already have given more thought to this question." He proceeded to deal with it.

One explanation, he suggested, was that "the nature of Communism has evolved in the Soviet Union. It has become less violently aggressive. The people have more diversity of opportunity." This development, he went on, "is a function of two things. First is the rising standard of living; and second is the increase of personal freedom." As the Soviet Union's power became "less monolithic" and as nuclear weapons became more frightening—and presumably because their use was less likely—the West had become less united. "I think," he said, "it's the military action we are taking alone which is the reason for so much dissatisfaction among intellectuals. The moral justification seems less and less convincing than when we were doing it in association with other nations."

Of course, McNamara said, these neo-isolationist ideas were being fed by misinformed people. He reached behind where he was sitting to pick up that morning's *Washington Post,* and he read to me from Walter Lippmann's column. In it, Lippmann quoted Hanson Baldwin, the military editor of *The New York Times,* to the effect that the United States did not have the ready strength to fulfill its foreign policy commitments. With unfeigned anger McNamara said that Baldwin was using the same arguments as "the militarists in the country."

McNamara then criticized John B. Oakes, the Editorial page editor of *The New York Times* for having said in editorials—in McNamara's words—that "the United States cannot afford to fulfill its foreign policy commitments." McNamara went on: "People ought to know how strong the United States is." Just think, he said, we have three hundred thousand men in combat without economic controls and without calling up the reservists. He called this accomplishment "unbelievable." General Westmoreland, he declared, could plan to drop in Vietnam this month ("he won't need to") two and a half times the average monthly tonnage dropped in Korea during the war there. Then he began to read to me from a paper in his pocket the specific figures—

astronomically large—for bombs, rockets, small arms ammunition, grenades, and mortar and artillery shells. He took care to say again that Westmoreland would not require all of this power. "I can't imagine he's gonna find targets to fire all this stuff at," was how he put it.

McNamara continued by saying that it was "absurd" to argue that the United States was "extended too thin" in the world. In this connection he mentioned that shortly after General James Gavin's letter expressing the idea that the United States was over-extended had appeared in *Harper's* magazine,* he had invited Gavin to come in to talk with him and presumably to argue with him. Again McNamara branded as foolish the idea that Americans, who were so affluent, could not afford their commitments, adding that, of course " 'shouldn't' is another thing."

People who argued that the United States ought to do less, overlook the fact that the Soviets were "still very aggressive," he said. "They are working in the Moslem world, pushing Egypt against Israel. The Middle East is just tinder dry. The Soviet Union is stirring things up. They are not seeking to make a nuclear assault because they know that that will produce no winners but they are probing politically to see if any military weakness shows up. The danger to the West is great and real." And apparently to make his point stronger, he said, "I am not myself one who gets scared at the sight of a Communist."

There were two views of the world, he went on. In one the value of independent states everywhere was recognized; in the other, there were spheres of influence. Walter Lippmann— whose anti-Vietnam position was a constant irritation to the Administration—"has always been a sphere of influence man." And in that view, the United States did not belong in

* February, 1966, under the title "The Easy Chair—A Communication on Vietnam from General James M. Gavin."

Vietnam, for it was outside our sphere. McNamara said he had to admit that this view "has short range popular appeal; but it is wrong in the long range." One element making for neo-isolationism, he reiterated, was the fact that the action taken by the United States in Vietnam had been unilateral.

We turned to another theoretical subject. How, I asked, does the United States relate to Red China? Clearly, *this* question McNamara had already given his mind to. He answered without hesitation: We must obtain multilateral recognition of the threat China poses to India, the rest of Asia, and surrounding areas. "Multilateral organization must be brought about by the nations threatened," he insisted. He revealed he and Rusk had attempted within NATO to "get a dialogue started" on the problem of how to deal with Chinese expansion. "It is questionable whether we can do this alone," and he explained that he doubted whether such a policy would be "politically acceptable to the people." He went on, "We must try to get the other nations to see the threat to peace that China is." The nations must collectively ask and answer these questions: "Are the Chinese a threat? Are they getting a military capability? If they are, is it a threat? If it is, how do you respond?" He did not seem optimistic about the response of the other nations. "Japan," he asserted incredulously, "is psychopathically afraid of war. The Defense Minister is not even in the Cabinet."

Then I moved the conversation to the previous month's peace offensive. "Were you optimistic about its possible results?" He replied, "I was in favor of it. I thought it possible but not probable that it might be successful. It was one scene in a multi-act play. If you stop at the third, you'll never get to the tenth." It was important, he said, to test what the Soviets had been saying—which was that a permanent halt in the bombing of North Vietnam could lead to the opening of peace talks. Then he added soberly, "The Soviets would like us deflated, but the conflict must not endanger *them*."

CHINA'S ROLE

"Is there danger of a belligerent response by the Chinese to the steps we are taking in Vietnam?" I asked. "Hell, yes," he replied, "we are running a risk of war with China." He added quickly that America ran the same risk by the actions it took in Korea and in Taiwan. He made the point that Ball had also made, that the Chinese response was not likely to involve war "so long as we do not appear to be striking to overthrow the regime of North Vietnam but only limitedly and solely to support the people of South Vietnam in shaping their own destiny." He concluded: "The risk of unlimited war is not very great." He spoke harshly about people who would like to strike at China, describing them as "preemptive hawks."

I now reminded McNamara that when we had talked in June, he had said that we were not moving in the direction of fighting a "land war" in Asia. Did he still hold that opinion? Yes, there was no "overt land war" in process. He defined such a war as one in which substantial numbers of Chinese or North Vietnamese were to enter the fighting in units "under their own flags." Furthermore, he said, "I begrudge the loss of a single man, but the casualty rate of 250 to 300 men a month" does not betoken an "overt land war." Besides, he said, it would be "hard for the Chinese to get down there. We are better equipped to supply our troops in Vietnam than they could supply theirs, even though we are 10,000 miles away."

"Can you tell me, Mr. Secretary, how large a commitment of men is the United States prepared to make?" I bluntly inquired. "I can't answer that," was his response, changing it quickly to "I don't answer that." He discoursed on the 200,-000 troops then in Vietnam and on the enormous mobility and firepower of the American soldier. "The thing we prize most deeply," he said, "is not money but men. . . . We have multiplied the capability of our men. It's expensive in dollars, but cheap in life."

I then asked McNamara what the word victory—as many people, including Vice-President Humphrey, were using it—meant. He answered that he tried to avoid such words as "victory" or "win"—which he called "color words." He preferred the phrase "favorable settlement," he said. And how, I inquired, did he think a "favorable settlement" might be brought about? He replied that the North could cease "feeding the fires of subversion and aggression in South Vietnam, and the NLF would shrink its activity against the south and withdraw to live and fight another day. South Vietnam would gradually expand its control and shape the outcome."

Could China abide such a result? I asked. Yes, he answered, it could be charged against the Soviet Union which could be blamed for not having provided sufficient materiel. "If I were a leader of China I think I would recognize I could be stronger later. I would wait for another day," he concluded.

As I stood up to leave I asked McNamara if there was anything he had done in his five years as Secretary of Defense that he wished he had done differently. I was thinking of Vietnam but he quickly referred to the Bay of Pigs. *That,* he said, was "a serious error." President Kennedy had taken full responsibility, "but, damn it, I was in the room." There was no mistaking the depth of his feeling.

And what about the course of the decisions respecting Vietnam? "There should be a critique of the whole episode but it will be years before we reach it." The lessons, he said, were not as yet completely clear. Still, some of them were worth talking about already. For instance, it might be useful to study whether we should not have changed our objectives five years ago or whether we could not have moved toward them more effectively. He did not elaborate.

In saying good-bye, I remarked on the superb pictures of

the Matterhorn and the Sierra Nevadas that McNamara, an accomplished mountain climber, displayed on the walls of his office. McNamara smiled broadly and asked me if I was a climber, too. I could not tell him I was. He assured me that mountains are "a wonderful environment to be in."

In a little while, I was back in the State Department waiting for Dean Rusk. On a wall of the reception room in which I sat hung a small painting of an Italian village scene, with the Papal coat of arms, in gold, embedded in the frame—a gift from Pope Paul on his recent visit. I wondered idly what sort of paintings American leaders leave abroad on state visits.

Seated at his desk in his shirtsleeves when I entered his office, Rusk stood up to greet me with a cordial handshake. It was late in the afternoon and he invited me to join him in a drink. A former professor of government, Rusk retorted wryly to my opening remark. I said I was going to ask him an historian's questions, not a Senator's. "I'm not sure that what historians don't know won't hurt them," he said grinning.

I rejoined with a complimentary word about his presentation of the Administration's position before the Senate Committee on Foreign Relations the previous week. He quickly shifted the conversation to a by-product of the occasion— James Reston's suggestion in *The New York Times* that the Secretary had enunciated a "Rusk Doctrine," committing the nation to protect militarily more than forty countries. Rusk commented tartly, "I didn't vote for a single one of those commitments. Those guys did"—meaning the members of the Senate. And, he added, "When you go into an alliance you have to mean it."

Rusk, talking of his critics, emphasized that "one thing really hasn't gotten into their gizzards" and that is that this country means what it says it means. "If you abandon one commitment how do you expect us to persuade anybody else that our word is to be relied on?" he asked.

He stayed on the subject. "I saw Chairman Khrushchev threaten President Kennedy with war over Berlin. And President Kennedy responded, 'If that's what you want, okay, but it'll be a very cold winter.' " The Soviets, Rusk said, simply had to believe that war would be the result. The same requirement, he went on, had obtained at the time of the Cuban missile crisis. And it could have been "the most frightful kind of war," he said.

It is imperative, he went on, that "when President Johnson says 'you're not going to have Vietnam,' " he be believed. "If ever the other side concludes that a President does not mean what he says," Rusk declared impressively, "we're finished, we're dead."

Then, in a more relaxed tone, he added, "Most totalitarian countries make a mistake about what a democracy will do at the end of the day." They regard us "as sloppy people with our hands in our pockets." Hitler, he said, had made the same wrong judgment. Hanoi miscalculated too; they decided they could have a larger war with impunity.

I switched the discussion to my insistent question: What had happened to the internationalists of only a few years ago who were now saying that the United States ought not to be so heavily committed in the world. Rusk answered that liberal intellectuals had always made a distinction between fascism on the one hand and Communism (Marxism-Leninism) on the other. "They are more concerned about the Hitler-kind of problem." Then he said with fervor, "A certain kind of liberalism is jaded and cynical. . . . Don't ask me to call a man a liberal who wants to turn over to a totalitarian regime more than fourteen million South Vietnamese."

Rusk believed also, he said, that some people had made too much of the possibility of *détente* with the Soviet Union. People built hopes on the basis of the nuclear test-ban treaty, which "went far beyond realities." The treaty came only a few months after the missile crisis, he pointed out. "It was a great step, but it did not signal a change of heart in the Communist world." Many people had come to regard Khrushchev as "an affable old grandfather," he declared. But, clinching the point, "he was sixty-seven and a half when he put missiles in Cuba."

Rusk went on, saying in a concerned voice that because there was so much hope for a general peace, the war in Vietnam had come upon the public as "a rude shock." People wanted to put the problem out of sight. "People thought it would go away before it became a major 'do.'" Their feelings of frustration developed in part because "the problem itself arose ambiguously." The regiments "sneaked" into South Vietnam rather than marched across the border.

Rusk turned again to the critics of Administration policies. "Many of those people," he said, "are not disclosing their premises." Senator Morse says openly that, "South Vietnam is not worth the life of a single American soldier," but others, including *The New York Times,* do not give the basis of their position. They talk of creating enclaves, though "the buts [in their statements] add up to withdrawal."

We switched the conversation then to the subject of China, and its relationship to the war in Vietnam. The American people were worried, Rusk said. "They ought to be," he added ominously. Since 1945 the serious possibility of a bigger war lurked in every crisis, and he listed the places they arose in: Greece, Berlin, Korea, and Cuba. "If we leave the impression with the other side that we can't face that possibility, then we'll never settle these questions. . . . They will push us until we fall." As to a showdown with China, "I'd rather be in our shoes than theirs," he declared.

I next asked Rusk about the peace offensive. How optimistic were the men who participated in it? There were, he was sure, "no substantial hopes." But such hope as there was certainly was "substantial enough to keep it from being phony." He pointed out that beginning in June, 1961, the United

States had not been idle in seeking peace in Southeast Asia. In the last twelve months, he remarked, over 125 efforts had been made.* President Johnson, he reminded me, had called in his Baltimore speech of April, 1965, for "unconditional discussions."

Then Rusk reviewed the history of dealing with what he calls "the other side." In 1961 President Kennedy suggested to Khrushchev in Vienna that "we all get out of Laos." Khrushchev agreed," said Rusk, "but he would not include Vietnam in the agreement." Had he done so, Rusk said, the step "could have been a contribution to peace." Hanoi, in violation of the agreement, left its forces in Laos and later infiltrated them into South Vietnam. The Soviet Union, Rusk thought, had acted in good faith, but the split between Moscow and Peking was already having an effect on the chances for peace in that part of the world.

He discussed the bombing pause of the previous May. "By the third day we had the answers." Peking said "no" on the radio and Hanoi refused to receive our message. "Gromyko himself told me in Vienna," he said, "that the pause and the message were an 'insult.' " Nevertheless, afterwards, several countries in Eastern Europe were saying that the United States could not get talks started unless it stopped the bombing. "We tried to find out what would happen if we did," he said, "but we still received no answer."

The longer bombing pause just concluded, he said without anger, was "harshly and negatively" received. The other side simply said, "Recognize the NLF as the sole bargaining representative of South Vietnam, accept the Four Points, and get out." Rusk ruminated, then went on: "It is a mystery, though, why Hanoi did not make it difficult for us by issuing an ambiguous response of one kind or another to our offer."

As to the dramatic activity of the United States' diplomats during the New Year peace offensive, Rusk said the United

* See list in Appendix D.

States wanted its efforts for peace to be known to "world public opinion. Nobody knew we'd been doing these things before." He said, "Our efforts had to be known. We had no problem of contacts." But, he added ruefully, "Hanoi and Peking are not responsible to world public opinion."

The resumption of bombing was the unanimous decision of the President and his senior advisers, including the National Security Council. I had asked the question specifically. Rusk volunteered: "No President since Franklin Roosevelt has spent more time than President Johnson gnawing into difficult questions. The impression he sometimes gives of being impetuous on major issues is wrong." Rusk wanted me to be clear on this. Possibly thinking of George Ball's work in connection with the decision to resume bombing, Rusk said that Johnson appointed some people to be devil's advocates. Sometimes he "goes outside the government." Subsequently, Bill Moyers told me that the President often relied for this kind of help on Clark Clifford, Arthur Dean, and John McCloy.

China, however, was the lodestone—as it had been in my conversations all day—and we were drawn back to it. Rusk was sure that there was a "flash-point" in Sino-American relations and "both sides are being very careful. As for the United States, we don't want events to take over. At the moment, we don't see a movement of forces suggesting a substantial deployment of men in the south. . . . We have not confronted them with [the need for] an orgasm of decision-making," he said solemnly as he "knocked wood" on the edge of his desk. "We will be watchful."

I asked Rusk, as I had asked McNamara: "Mr. Secretary, are there some things with respect to Vietnam in the last five years that you wish had been done differently?" He answered, without hesitating, that after the Vienna meeting of June, 1961, we should have put down "a lot of blue chips immediately" to head off "misunderstanding by the other side" and to make crystal clear: "you can't have South Vietnam." But, he added, such steps would have coincided chronologically with the Berlin crisis and the fact that defense costs were already rising. Things would have turned out better if there had been "more, sooner, rather than less." During 1964 the Communists thought they needed only to find a way for the United States to save face, having concluded that this was what we wanted to do. They misunderstood: "We were not interested in saving face but in saving Vietnam."

THE WAR'S ENDING

Then I asked how he thought the war would end. Instantaneously, he replied, "It won't end at the UN." He went on, "They won't come to the table so long as they think they can get South Vietnam. If they decide they can't win, they may come to the conference table to see what they can get there." They may, he said, "just let things peter out, the way the Greek guerrillas did." This would result from the decision on their part to stop and wait for another day. (McNamara had also implied the same possibility, leading me to regard this projection as an important assumption guiding the Administration.) "We could get back faster than they. We could get back our lines of communication in a fashion far superior to theirs."

Rusk predicted, moreover, that the denouement in Vietnam could come suddenly. He recalled for me how unexpectedly and cryptically the word had reached the United States years ago that the Soviet Union was ready to lift the blockade of Berlin. Stalin, he said, had delivered a diatribe against the Western powers occupying Berlin. Ambassador Philip Jessup met Soviet Ambassador Jacob Malik at the bar of the UN and Jessup, acting on instructions, asked Malik casually if Stalin's omission of the currency question from his usual calendar of Western sins had any significance. Malik answered that he did not know, but that he would try to find out. The following week, he told Jessup that indeed the omission did have significance. "What significance?" asked Jessup. "I'll find out," Malik responded, and shortly negotiations were commenced. I felt pleased by this illustration of the evident usefulness of history, but also uncomfortable because the analogy seemed so neat and clear-cut.

"The other side is hurting," Rusk observed. The signs were increasing; he listed some of them: the Vietcong and the North Vietnamese lost more men in 1965 than the United States lost in the entire Korean War; prisoners told that Ho Chi Minh's statement about being ready to fight a ten- or twenty-year war had had a depressing effect on morale; the other side could not keep a battalion of troops in combat more than twenty-four hours because of the intense firepower to which they were exposed; there was no rest for their soldiers, who had always to be on the move; defections had increased fourfold. Rusk said he drew a conclusion from these facts: "On the present basis they are not going to come out of it." I asked him whether he had anticipated the present escalation of the war into a "land war." "This is not the great land war that people talk about," he replied with some annoyance, explaining that "you can't find the enemy."

Of course, he went on before I could interrupt, an important question was, "What are the big brothers going to do?" The evidence was that they were "more cautious in action than in words. It's a tough game we're playing and we could be wrong," he warned. And he added quickly: "The President cannot rely on a guess on this subject. Everybody can say, 'Sorry boss, I was wrong,' except him." "Can China abide the defeat of North Vietnam?" I interjected. "Yes," he replied. "They've suffered an even more disastrous blow in Indonesia."

Those who made policy, Rusk continued, can "draw no doctrinal conclusion about what the other side will *not* do.

89

Decisions have to be based on all contingencies and all consequences of various alternatives. . . . If the other side is as concerned as they ought to be in similar fashion, maybe we'll get some peace out of it at some point."

I raised the notion that critics and editorial writers had been hammering into the public mind, namely that "new" ideas for ending the war ought to be introduced into the scene. Rusk bristled somewhat as he responded: "If a man has one idea in a lifetime he's done pretty damn well. The really great ideas are rather rare." He continued, "And how rare is the idea [in foreign affairs] that has not been investigated and examined in this Department." He defined a "great" idea as "one on which no improvement can be made," for example, Thomas Jefferson's idea that government must rest on the consent of the governed. Rusk concluded: "Teatime table conversation that plays around with whatever is on the tip of the tongue doesn't add much in this kind of business." Then he reflected for a minute on the fact that the United States was subjected to a double standard on how it performed in the world. (He meant, I assumed, that the performance of the nation was always being compared with its high ideals.) The Soviet Union, on the other hand—he said he was quoting Ambassador Charles ("Chip") Bohlen—"enjoys the dividends of bastardy."

As I raised questions about the widespread opposition on Capitol Hill to the Administration's Vietnam policy, Rusk switched back to the hearings of the Senate Committee on Foreign Relations. He said that the Committee seldom had a quorum for its private sessions, implying that the Committee was in full attendance only when the television cameras were on. Senator Fulbright, he said, was an "intuitive maverick," which "makes for complications in the chairmanship of a committee." He continued, "I knew him at Oxford," recalling the time in the 1930's when both had been Rhodes scholars. "He never agreed with anybody." With some heat, Rusk stated that Fulbright said we ought to offer "the other side" something. Yet, Rusk declared, looking me straight in the eye, "nobody is offering us anything. If the other side wants peace we will be in Geneva tomorrow afternoon to talk." Rusk seemed to sum up his feelings about the Administration's plight as he said resignedly, "We're caught between the hawks and the doves."

We turned from the cosmic events to other matters; we talked of Rusk's personal future. Was he going to write his memoirs? I asked. No, he said with certainty. But he also said he might write on particular problems such as "the Press and the conduct of foreign relations." No, he was not going to write his memoirs, he repeated. "I have a strong conviction that people who deal in confidences with each other should keep those confidences." He said this with irate vehemence. "If Kennedy had known what Schlesinger and Sorensen were going to write, he would not have kept them at what they were doing. Schlesinger wrote that I 'sat like a Buddha at meetings.' When he was in the same room, I sure as hell did!"

Rusk said he might decide to write some anecdotal accounts of various events in the Department of State that he had been witness to: "Anecdotal material is priceless" in interpreting certain pivotal public actions, he explained.

As I stood up to go, I asked him why Indochina, where the Japanese-American War began in 1941, continued to be an American sticking point. He smiled and reminisced that when he was in charge of intelligence in the China–Burma–India theater during the Second World War, he received permission to inquire "through channels" as to what President Roosevelt's post-war plans for the region were. Many months later Roosevelt's answer—along with answers to other questions—came back across the Pacific: "I don't want to hear any more about Indochina!" I offered the prediction that if that story was a sample of what might be in an anecdotal history of great decisions, the book would be a best seller.

The next morning I had appointments at the White House to see McGeorge Bundy and then the President. Arriving early, I drank coffee with Hayes Redmon. Redmon had helped prepare certain memoranda on Vietnam for the President.

Knowing that Redmon had contributed to the making of the decision the previous December that halted the bombing, I asked him to discuss the peace offensive as a whole. He told me of the direct contacts with Hanoi's people that were made in Moscow and in Vientiane and of one contact that was made through a go-between in Rangoon. In each instance, he said, the rebuff by the North Vietnamese had been complete. In Moscow, Redmon said, at the second contact the North Vietnamese representative handed the United States Ambassador Hanoi's familiar four points. Nevertheless, the State Department instructed the Ambassador to see the representative once again and ask him, "Have you anything more from your government?" Again a negative. Redmon's words stuck in my mind: "We really tried. We gave them every chance in the world."

I broke off the conversation on being told that Bundy was free. Bundy said hello cheerily, prefacing it with a remark about "peace having broken out." The reference was unfortunately not to Vietnam, but to our earlier disagreement.*

Just as we began the conversation, Bundy telephoned Senator Robert Kennedy. Bundy talked for a minute about the apparent disagreement between Kennedy and the Administration over Vietnam policy that Kennedy had expressed the day before. "The matter is covered," I heard

* See p. 49.

Bundy say, and he ended the brief conversation with the words, "love you, Bobby."

I asked Bundy what he thought Vice-President Humphrey meant in Asia when he spoke of "victory." Bundy replied that of course he could not comment on anything the Vice-President said. But he indicated that the word meant "preventing a take-over in Vietnam through various kinds of force." Success was possible in Vietnam, Bundy went on, "and the chances of getting it have gone up in the last year." As to the idea that "there is no substitute for victory," Bundy said blandly, "Johnson is not MacArthur; he is not Goldwater."

Bundy said he believed that a take-over by the Vietcong was not what the people of South Vietnam wanted. He thought it significant that Premier Ky's government contained former members of the Viet Minh who had broken with the Communist party. Indeed, he was quick to point out, the South Vietnamese Ambassador in Washington had once been a member of the Viet Minh. "There are none so blind," he wound up, "as those who will not see."

I asked the question uppermost in my recent reflections: What had happened to the liberals, who only a while ago were earnest supporters of America's involvement in the world? Bundy seized on the topic. Liberals, he said, had no trouble opposing Hitler, but Communism was another matter. He mentioned the Truman Doctrine applied to Greece, and said that Henry Wallace and Archibald MacLeish, liberals both, opposed it. "People should have believed some things sooner," he said in a matter-of-fact tone.

As to Vietnam, "It's the part of the world we're in, and it's the steaming jungle." The liberals, he said, "never learned internationalism with respect to Asia. "If Kennedy were doing it [that is, waging war in Vietnam], they'd be less distressed." With President Johnson in the White House, "they feel a strain. . . . He's a tough Texan who is honestly scary." But, Bundy went on, "he's got his fist in the dike." Bundy clinched his point: "The aggression in Vietnam is less clear-cut than in Korea and so it does not force a moral judgment as it did then. This helps our liberal friends cover their shame."

PACIFICATION

We then talked about what was being called the third phase of the war—the economic and social phase. Bundy called it "a new emphasis on an old theme." He spoke of the enormous importance of "the civil side of the war." I asked him how it was going and I observed that the newspaper accounts I read were contradictory. "Ask the President," he shot back, leading me to believe that the President would have an optimistic report. "The military side is going better," he volunteered—"where we can bring them to battle." Yet, he said, although the morale of the other side had been hurt, South Vietnam still had a high rate of desertion in its army and still suffered from attacks by terrorists.

I asked about the role our allies were playing. He replied, "We cannot say we won't fight without our allies. The G.I.'s don't ask 'Where are the Koreans?' " He mentioned the contribution of the Filipinos, just then about to send combat engineers, and of the South Koreans. The Thais, he said, are "deeply engaged." The Australians and the New Zealanders had more troops there than they had a year ago. But language was a problem where troops of various countries were together.

"Is it a 'land war' in Asia?" I asked. He thought a moment: "It is less than a full-scale war and more than a guerrilla war. It is being fought in the shelter of sea and air power. All of South Vietnam is an enclave; the populated area is all accessible from the sea—that's what's wrong with Gavin's position."

We talked about China for a few minutes. "What would be the critical point at which China would enter the fighting?" China, he replied, could abide the collapse of the North Vietnamese military effort in the South. Moscow, too, could live with such a collapse, because the Soviet Union had invested but little prestige there. "We are always concerned about a direct conflict with the Chinese. We are always engaged in 'China-watching' just as we are engaged in 'Soviet Union-watching.' So far, the words of the Chinese are wilder than their actions." But, he added temperately, they "might make a bad decision" in following what they regard as their best interest.

The making of peace, however, was as much on Bundy's mind as the possibility of a bigger war. We discussed the peace offensive. Why did we conduct it so flamboyantly? I wanted to know. We had two objectives, was Bundy's quick rejoinder. "We wanted to make it clear we are communicating. And heads of government like it that way." Bundy expanded the second point. "Lyndon Johnson sent word direct. Wilson likes to get into the act by getting the poop from Goldberg. We like to get the word direct, too."

Did he think that the peace offensive was still going on? Not all of the responses, he said, had "surfaced" yet. "We continue to talk to people." Bundy emphasized that the peace offensive was not based on the notion that "damn it, if only you say the right thing you could turn the key in the lock." But he was firm: the President "insists on making sure we miss no opportunity to show we are trying."

"Could the United Nations help?" I asked. Bundy's response surprised me by its intensity. "U Thant is a neutralist. He does not believe China is a problem and Burma [U Thant's native country] is not involved." The neutral's point of view is "let's you and him fight," he continued. "I don't blame the neutrals," he added in a monotone, and he compared them with "the knowledgeable Swiss in Hitler's war."

I then turned to the matter of the resumption of the bombing. The attacks had to be resumed, Bundy said sharply. "If you stop to give people a chance, you don't just stop it permanently. It would lead to a conclusion by Hanoi that if they kept up the propaganda barrage they could get the whole thing called off."

We were interrupted by a phone call about the speech the President was to deliver that night at Freedom House in New York. Bundy told his caller that he had already talked to George Ball about the sentence which read "Hanoi will not impose upon the people of South Vietnam a government not of their choice." I overheard Bundy say, "Yes, 'shall not' is better than 'will not,' because it's not a prediction but an assertion of purpose." *

We were soon talking again. I felt obliged to ask what were the lessons he had learned in the five years he had spent in the White House. His ready reply was a summary of experience: "In 1961 we were overwhelmed by work; we had to learn on the fly." He was certain, he said, that he was now "less impatient with procedures." Some things require "methodical clearance," he declared. "You must get used to this job before you can cut corners."

I told Bundy I was on my way to talk to the President. He offered the idea, generally shared in the White House, that the President's gall bladder operation had been a "great thing" for the President. He was stronger, more at ease, more buoyant, and more good-humored, Bundy reported. I told him I hoped to verify that report. I wished Bundy well

* The final version of the address is in *Public Papers of the Presidents of the United States: Lyndon B. Johnson, 1966*, Book I (Washington, 1967), pp. 208–15.

The Tuesday Cabinet in session—May 16, 1967—in the President's Dining Room, its regular meeting place. Clockwise from President Johnson are Robert S. McNamara, Secretary of Defense; General Earle G. Wheeler, Chairman of the Joint Chiefs of Staff; George E. Christian, White House Press Secretary; Walt W. Rostow, Presidential Assistant for National Security Affairs; Vice President Hubert H. Humphrey (not a member); Richard M. Helms, Director of the Central Intelligence Agency; Dean Rusk, Secretary of State. *(White House Photograph)*

Another view of the Tuesday Cabinet at work, later in 1967. Clockwise from President Johnson are McNamara; Christian; Rostow; W. Thomas Johnson, Assistant Press Secretary; Helms; Rusk. Wheeler is absent. *(White House Photograph)*

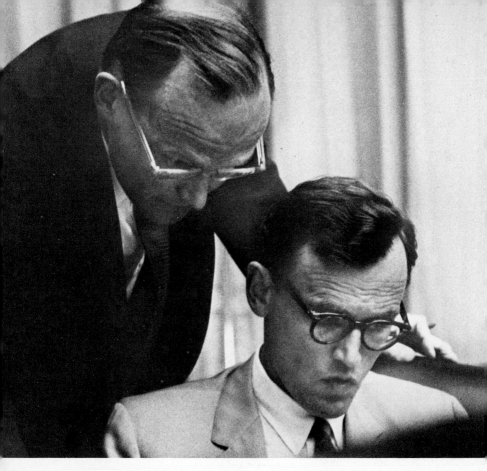

A charter member of the Tuesday Cabinet was McGeorge
Bundy, Rostow's predecessor as Assistant to the President for
National Security Affairs. Here in the Cabinet Room of the
White House he peers over the shoulder of his brother, Wil-
liam P. Bundy, Assistant Secretary of State for Far Eastern
Affairs. *(White House Photograph)*

Another member of the first Tuesday Cabinet was Bill D. Moyers, Special Assistant to the President and Press Secretary. He is shown in the Cabinet Room taking notes on McNamara's words after an evening meeting as the President and General Wheeler pay close attention. *(White House Photograph)*

President Johnson and his advisers listen on January 25, 1966, to Senator J. William Fulbright of Arkansas (back to camera), the chief opponent of their policy on Vietnam. Facing the the camera are, l. to r., Rusk, the President, McGeorge Bundy, and McNamara. Directly behind the President is George W. Ball, Undersecretary of State. *(White House Photograph)*

General Wheeler, late on October 31, 1968, issues the order to halt the bombing of North Vietnam. He is using a phone in the President's "little office" adjoining the Oval Office. The three framed documents are the ones referred to in the text. *(White House Photograph)*

One of the last meetings of the Tuesday Cabinet. Clark L. Clifford, having succeeded McNamara as Secretary of Defense sits in his place at the table. Clockwise from the President are Clifford, Wheeler, Rostow, Tom Johnson, and Rusk. *(Stan Wyman, LIFE Magazine © Time Inc.)*

in his new duties as President of the Ford Foundation—
the appointment had recently been announced—and I left.

My date with the President had been pushed forward a
little by the fact that his breakfast with the Congressional
leaders had run somewhat longer than planned. I sat a few
minutes waiting in the Cabinet room. Idly I studied the four
portraits that adorned the walls—Jefferson, Webster, Jackson, and Franklin Roosevelt (the last directly facing the President's chair). I also admired Felix de Weldon's splendid
sculptured head of Kennedy, done in 1963.

Marvin Watson then came to the door and escorted me to
the Oval Office. The President was in a pleasant mood. He
welcomed me, leading the way into what he had called, the
last time I saw him, his "little office," a place to which he
could retreat, just off his main office. He asked if he could
get me a drink—a Coke or a Dr. Pepper—as he was having
one. I took a Coke and sat on the small sofa. The President took the easy chair opposite. Bill Moyers, who had
joined us, sat in a corner.

Moyers and the President and—on the intercom—Harry
McPherson, another assistant, spoke for a few minutes among
themselves about the letter Johnson would quote from in
his Freedom House address. It was from Merriman Smith,
then the senior White House newspaper correspondent, whose
son had been killed in a helicopter accident in Vietnam a
few days earlier. Johnson said, "I can't read it without cry-
ing. I didn't think I could get through yesterday" (when
the letter apparently had arrived).

The President turned to me, his mind still on the American soldiers in Vietnam, and began to talk. He was very
proud, he said, that we had moved between 150,000 and
200,000 men into Vietnam with "the greatest efficiency in
the history of the world." He spoke of the military hospitals
that had been built and of the housing waiting for our men
when they arrived. General Westmoreland, he said, had called

97

our army "the most mobile under any flag, the best equipped, and the one with the most firepower per man." The President had asked him if he was short of anything and the General had replied that he was short of nothing that affected the fighting. (The only complaints the President knew of were a shortage of beer, that McGeorge Bundy had found when he was there, and the price of cigarettes.)

The President returned to thoughts of the casualties. "We have," he said, "the lowest ratio of wounded to dead we've ever had—three to one." By using helicopters, he said, it was possible to transport a man from the battlefield to a hospital in from thirty minutes to an hour. He had praise not only for the medical services but also for the search-and-rescue units that picked up the wounded.

Then Johnson alluded to the Vietcong losses. He said the Vietcong had suffered 30,000 casualties in two months, out of a population of 14,000,000—a ratio staggering to the mind. (I took his statement to mean in the previous two months.) "Think of how terrible it would be if our losses were proportionately as high as theirs. We don't think Hanoi knows how serious it is," he observed gravely. "They are looking at things through rose-colored glasses, intoxicated on the Senate hearings." In an aside, the President chided me and my colleagues. "You professors," he said, "are just as bad." When I protested, he talked of how the Kaiser and Hitler, too, had misinterpreted the will of America.

Reading as he spoke, the President handed me his weekly cable just arrived from Ambassador Lodge in Saigon. "Here," he said, "you read it. I haven't read it yet. You're a patriot." (I assumed he meant I was a loyal citizen.) The report was labeled "Secret Nodis" (Nodis is government language for "not to be distributed.") It summarized for the President the important intelligence of the week. It contained, among other items, the information that some

Vietcong machine-gunners had been found dead manacled to their weapons. The report also said that Lodge had had lunch with elements of the First Cavalry Division and that one soldier had told him he found it easier to understand the draft-card burners than "the prominent men of the Senate who decided to put on this hearing." (The reference was to the hearings held the previous week by the Senate Committee on Foreign Relations.)

While I was reading, the President was again talking over the intercom with McPherson, this time relating a humorous political anecdote to illustrate a point. As soon as I had finished the cable, the President turned and said, "There have been opponents in every war. But there is more unanimity today than in the past."

With unabashed satisfaction, the President then talked about the hopes he had for the Asia Development Bank about to be created. "Germany and England held back," he said, but "I got hold of them personally."

He returned again to his critics on Asia. He spoke particularly and with sadness about Senator Fulbright. His mind was on the place of television in disseminating criticism. "When Fulbright drops a pen in the Senate, it can be seen instantaneously in Johnson City. Why, it took three days to hear from the post office when I was a boy."

FULBRIGHT'S STAND

I asked the President how he explained Fulbright's opposition. "It's some little racial problem." Fulbright, who had studied at Oxford simply "cannot understand that people with brown skins value freedom too. I say," added the President, clearly as if it were not for the first time, "if you want a social revolution in the Dominican Republic, why don't you start it in Little Rock?" The allusion was to Fulbright's

99

denunciation of United States' armed intervention in 1965 and his stand on desegregation in his home state in 1956.

Fulbright, the President went on, had opposed wage and hour legislation, had favored the Dixon-Yates contract, was against the poverty program, and had voted against every civil-rights bill. "Some people say he votes against civil-rights bills because that's the only way he can get elected in Arkansas. I'll tell you why he votes against civil rights: he's against civil rights!

"I had proposed him to President Kennedy as Secretary of State. But the Africans would be opposed. Bobby and the President decided it wouldn't go." He reminisced some more: "Fulbright once said that President Truman ought to resign. Later, he made fun of Eisenhower; he thought Eisenhower was a boob."

Fulbright, the President kept on, voted for the SEATO Treaty—under the provisions of which the United States defended its engagement in Vietnam, while "neither Kennedy nor I did," adding, "we were sick at the time." ("I didn't make this contract," he said later in our conversation.) "The Vietcong have more negotiators and advisers with me than [I have] American soldiers," he said with irritation. As to the critics, he asked, "Who the hell are they representing?"

Then he told how he had gone to Congress for the resolution of support in August, 1964, informing the lawmakers, "They just shot at my destroyer and I shot back." He explained how he had helped give Eisenhower a similar resolution to protect Formosa. He continued calmly, "I've inherited this thing and I'm there. I want Congress to go with me. They were there for the takeoff; I want them there for the landing. I think we're doing pretty well."

But his anger over the Senate hearings was apparent. He harked back to Fulbright—"a frustrated old woman," and "the hero of the Oxford intellectuals. We here at the White

House have to call people to attend his committee meetings sometimes when he has no quorum." *

"Mr. President," I asked, "how do you account for the opposition to the fighting—Senatorial and other?" He replied that there was a strong strain of racism in it, by which he meant a feeling that the Vietnamese "are not our kind of people, that they're an ancient people, that they're brown people, not able to take care of themselves."

The President's patent annoyance dissipated as he said that he was "not angry or upset. Our people are moving," he declared, "and theirs [the enemy's] are not." And he added wistfully, "I'm opening every peace door I can."

Returning to the subject of the Senate hearings, he complained: the members of the committee had come up with "no plan, no program, no idea. They labored and brought forth three ex-Ambassadors: [Maxwell] Taylor, [George] Kennan, and [James] Gavin. Gavin was so bad as Ambassador to France we had to remove him;** and Kennan admitted he had never been in southeast Asia and didn't know what the hell he was talking about."† (He pronounced the name

* Puzzled by such an unusual report, I subsequently learned a possible explanation for it: On one occasion when Fulbright and other senators were out of town on the campaign trail, the Administration wanted to bring out of committee a bill involving the International Development Association. On its own, the Treasury Department urged certain members of the Foreign Relations Committee to attend a meeting in order to help make a quorum.

** Gavin had been appointed to Paris by President Kennedy in 1961. Gavin resigned the following year, citing a desire to return to private business (*The New York Times,* Aug. 1, 1962).

† Kennan, a former Ambassador to the Soviet Union, had begun his testimony: "I would like to explain, in undertaking to speak on this subject, that southeast Asia is a part of the world for which I can claim no specialized knowledge." *Supplemental Foreign Assistance, Fiscal Year 1966—Vietnam: Hearings before the Committee on Foreign Relations, United States Senate, Eighty-ninth Congress, Second Session . . .* Part 1 (Washington, 1966), p. 331.

101

Kennan, "keen-in"—deliberately, I thought, in order to be more disdainful.)

Once more, the President talked about the coming of the Second World War, and how "we had to stop Hitler even though many people thought we could be Fortress America." With Fulbright still on his mind, he added, "Oxford didn' recognize the danger till the Battle of Britain. Fulbright feels racist." And as the President was seeming to follow his stream of consciousness, he pointed out that Negroe "are only 11 percent of the population. But 22 percent of the troops in South Vietnam are Negro."

Going on, he repeated: "I didn't make this contract SEATO." He talked for a minute about how Dulles was determined to halt aggression. As he spoke, he pulled up his trouser leg, adjusted his sock, and scratched. He continued: "Eisenhower told Kennedy, 'Vietnam and Laos wil be your biggest problems.' After Kennedy became President people began to say 'Whatever happened to Lyndon?' I wa the number two man, of course, but the real number two man was Bobby Kennedy." He proceeded: "It was Presiden Kennedy"—the meaning being Kennedy-without-Johnson—"who said, 'We're here till we win.' "

Johnson talked of his conviction. "A gangster cannot gob ble up a Rockefeller by force," was his formulation. He turned to his critics again: "They don't have the courage to say 'Let's get out.' " He excepted only Senator Morse who he said, had three times declared that the United State must get out. "The Committee could have recommended that we withdraw, that we accept the enclave idea, that we bomb North Vietnam harder, or that we strike China with nuclear weapons. But all they keep saying is, 'We're going to get into a war with China.' "

The President then seemed to be thinking aloud as he said, "Why would the Chinese want to take on the United States of America? We could take out those eleven target in seventeen minutes.* It would be like an eleven-year-old colored girl from Tennessee going up against Jack Dempsey."

The President anticipated my next question—What are the chances that China will come in?—and went on, "I don't think anybody knows. I'm no expert. Of course, if I spit in her face and get close that's one thing, but if I don't, most say she won't. In the meantime, though, what are we supposed to do—hide and lie in fear? Who in the hell is the Big Bad Wolf?"

In past crises—over Iran, Berlin, and Cuba—people were not "going around asking, 'Are we going to get into a war with Russia?' One way to avoid it [a war with China] is to quit talking about it."

Then the President took up the public opinion polls. A solid ten percent, he said, "want to go hot-headed—Goldwater types"; ten percent "are ready to run"; twenty percent are for more bombing; sixty percent say "we are doing right." He pulled out of his pocket the latest polls showing that my own Congressional District, the 25th of New York —"Ottinger's," he called it,** conformed almost exactly to the national profile.

This led him again to pose a question and answer it: When is the war going to be over? "When Churchill said we'll fight 'em on the beaches and in the alleys, he didn't say when he'd be done. When MacArthur came out of the Philippines with his head down, and left Skinny Wainwright behind, Roosevelt didn't say 'I'll get you out by Thanksgiving.' If Fulbright makes me testify on this one, I'll have to take the Fifth Amendment."

But the President tried to answer the question for me anyhow. General Westmoreland he reported as being most

---

* Probably a reference to a list of military targets he had seen and discussed.
** He was speaking of Representative Richard L. Ottinger (Democrat).

optimistic. "He says the war cannot last many years." Th
North Vietnamese casualties are very heavy. The defection
are doubling—"averaging seventeen hundred a month, wit
two thousand this month." He interjected, "After the Alamo,
"no one thought Sam Houston would wind it up so quick.
And then he mused, "Who knows how long, how much. Th
important thing is, are we right or wrong?"

SOUTH VIETNAM'S FUTURE

I broke in to ask about the new phase of the war. His fac
lit up. "The war is two-pronged," he said. He made tw
fists. He thrust one forward signifying the military side an
then the other signifying the economic and social side. Thi
second was the side he plainly *wanted* to talk about. H
said proudly, "I want to leave the footprints of Americ
there. I want them to say, 'when the Americans come, thi
is what they leave—schools, not long cigars.' " He paused
"We're going to turn the Mekong into a Tennessee Valley.

The President spoke of the average income of the Vie
namese—"65 dollars a year." They need schools, healtl
measures, and agricultural assistance. "We're going to teacl
'em to read and write," he said with elation. He explaine
that the United States was transmitting television program
from a plane over South Vietnam. He said the cooks a
Lodge's house, looking at TV for the first time, were wide
eyed in amazement. The President rose partly out of hi
chair, his own eyes wide and with arms raised and ou
stretched in front of him to show how the cooks probabl
looked. Then as he settled into the chair again he said softly
"I remember the first time I heard radio."

Back to present measures, the President said he was askin
Ambassador William Porter to serve in the economic an
social field as a counterpart to General Westmoreland. Th
work of uplifting South Vietnam, he said, "is tough. You buil

schools and hospitals and they shoot them up." What about Premier Ky? Ky, the President said with delight, "sounded like Rex Tugwell." I asked him what he meant by that and he recalled that in the early days of the New Deal, Rexford G. Tugwell had said that we must "roll up our sleeves and remake America." *

Never once, the President said, had he and Ky discussed a troop buildup. "And I never had a conversation with him in which I tried to make him sit down with the Vietcong." The President asserted that reporters hounded Ky to get him to say something he did not want to say. (The President described one well-known newspaperman as having gone after Ky like "a great big Dane dog.") The President mocked the news reports that said he and Ky had parted because Ky "wouldn't sit down with the Vietcong." As to the Vietcong, Johnson said soberly, "We'll work out a way to hear them. But we've found out all over that when you bring the Communists in, they chew you up."

He returned to the subject of the South Vietnamese. "They have 700,000 men fighting. We're not giving them up." He insisted, "We're fighting for a limited objective. We don't want to do a damn thing to China or North Vietnam. We just want to have them leave these people alone." He reminded himself of an analogy: years earlier Huey Long had gone into Arkansas to campaign for Hattie Caraway for the Senate.** The President told the story of the campaign with zest and amusing detail; Long was merely protecting Mrs. Caraway, who was otherwise helpless, against Arkansas Power and Light, which the President described

* Tugwell was a Columbia economist who became one of Franklin D. Roosevelt's Brain Trusters and helped frame the Agricultural Adjustment Act of 1933.
** Mrs. Caraway, the first woman to be a United States Senator, was appointed to her late husband's seat in 1931. The following year she won her first full term after defeating six male opponents in the Democratic primary. She was defeated in the 1944 primary by J. W. Fulbright.

as having been in those days "thieving sons of bitches." Th
little person, he said, had about as much chance again
them as "an Arab in the Jewish district of New York."

The United States' strategy is "not to destroy or kill bu
simply to stop them from bringing the stuff down into th
south. One of the things in war," he stated, "is fear." Genera
Eisenhower, he said, had advised him, "Tell 'em they hav
no sanctuary." Eisenhower had also told him, he saic
that he had called in Nehru during the Korean War to as
him to tell "them": "We don't have these weapons just t
be stored. And they said 'uh-oh.' "

Johnson repeated his main ideas. "They must stop thei
aggression. If they'll go home tomorrow, I'll go home th
next day. . . . We are not fussing the Chinese peopl
We're not trying to get them into trouble. We've sent n
plane close to their border." He summed up: "The hearing
not Lyndon Johnson, have excited all this talk." He change
his tone and startled me as he said, "I ask how many time
do I let a fiend rape my wife?" Then his voice softened an
he said, "I'm just trying to make a point you won't forget.
Then he flayed Fulbright once more, this time for arguin
that "the more you debate, the better." Said Johnso
"That's a lot of crap."

As the meeting ended, the President stood up and accom
panied me to the vestibule of his office. In good humor (Bund
was right) he bade me good-bye.

I went to lunch with Bill Moyers in the White Hous
staff mess. As we sat down, I asked Moyers to tell me mor
about the President's view of his critics. Moyers answere
that the President did not, of course, want to constrain o
silence criticism. And this meant, naturally, that he uphel
Fulbright's right to conduct hearings.

But Johnson disagreed with what he took as Fulbright
"pathological defeatism" regarding Asia. The President, ac
cording to Moyers, thought that Fulbright was too much Eu

rope-oriented and too inclined to believe that white people were alien to the cultures of Asia and therefore had no role and no future there. Moyers went on: "The President has tried hard to accommodate himself to his critics. He had a short bombing pause; he acknowledged a role for the Vietcong; he had a long bombing pause; he took the issue to the UN; he called for a gigantic political and social effort in Vietnam. . . . The President would like to know why he is sometimes called dogmatic and doctrinaire when in fact it is the others who are dogmatic and doctrinaire."

Moyers detailed how carefully the President worked toward the conclusions he reached. He spoke of the roles of Clark Clifford, Arthur Dean, and John McCloy. "As lawyers they dissect the case in question from every angle."

Then Moyers explained the rationale of the decision to resume the bombing. "The absence of bombing would free the other side's hand more than we would like to see," he said. "The bombing has restricted the size of the force that can be supported in the South." But, "the overriding reason is political: to put pressure on Hanoi and China. It will disabuse them of the idea that they can have a privileged sanctuary if they are going to sustain their aggression."

The halt "carried repressed hopes about the intransigence of the other side. The repressed hopes breathed a little fresh air," he said. "The other side shut the window quickly."

"Why," I asked, "*did* 'the other side' respond this way?" I posed this question because an interpretation of this fact seemed as important as any other single consideration in understanding the Administration's position. "The other side," Moyers answered, "is convinced that they shall prevail, that they have more patience in the bank than we do." Yet, he continued, they "must recognize the inevitability of the outcome. That is why it's wrong to pressure the President to accommodate to their position."

On the subject of the Senate hearings, Moyers referred to

George Kennan's ignorance of China and of Asia in general. His knowledge of that part of the world, Moyers said, "would fit in a keyhole." Yet Moyers did not dismiss the hearings as unimportant. The President, he said, was certain that "no one can now say the policy has not been scrutinized. Having heard *no* rational alternative, the President can now prosecute it with all his energy." The President "has a new conviction that we can see this thing through, that limited objectives with maximum resources can prevail." Moyers listed the objectives: "One, to frustrate aggression against one state by another; two, to disabuse aggressors of the use of force; three, to force them into a posture of negotiations and compromise."

I asked what the President and his men believed China's response would be in the long run?

"China," said Moyers, "will tolerate an end to the war of liberation, but probably not the obliteration of North Vietnam. The closer we get to the border, the more uncertain we are. . . . The fear is of an irrational response by China—a blind reaction to exterior influences. The President wants to avoid giving China a reason for coming into war with the United States. He can't gamble on their poor judgment." Moyers concluded: "China cannot take peace in Asia for granted—not at any cost, not at the cost of liberty-loving people, not at the cost of yielding to aggression."

It was plainly impossible for me to list in systematic order the multitudinous impressions I gained from these conversations. Nevertheless, I could enumerate a few salient points.

The most important was that those who made the country's policy were neither tired nor discouraged. They were hopeful, even though not enthusiastic about the bombing pause and the peace offensive, self-assured but not cocky. Their willingness to look for instruction and guidance from their opponents in Congress and in the nation was unimpaired. Seeing these men just after the Senate hearings, I found them in full command of their abilities.

The course of this uniquely frustrating war had not turned them into vindictive warriors. They had no doubt about America's physical power, but they did not lose sight of the country's role as a humane force, too. At one point the President said to me with obvious distress that India might lose as many people by starvation that year as the whole population of Vietnam. He added: "I'm going to try to help them."

When I had last seen the President and his close advisers they were waiting for a word from Hanoi or Peking that the hour for negotiations had struck. They were still waiting, but after their fruitless efforts to move to the conference table, they were now emboldened, it seemed to me, by the fact that the onus of guilt for the continuation of the war was on the other side. This was what enabled them to face their critics with equanimity. They had been forced by the enemy to believe that a military solution was a livelier possibility than a political or diplomatic solution.

☆ ☆ ☆ ☆ ☆ ☆

In early March, 1966, Secretary McNamara announced that 30,000 more troops would shortly be sent to South Vietnam. The total would then be 235,000. He said that General Westmoreland would probably request more men in the near future. Meanwhile, it was reported that between January 1 and March 1 the United States had suffered 4,300 casualties (640 killed).

The Saigon government had yet to demonstrate that it commanded the widespread support of its people. A Buddhist monk, Thich Tri Quang, was leading a vigorous anti-government campaign in Hue and Danang. In response to

this and other agitation Premier Ky promised that election
would take place late in the year, which would prove the
extent and success of the "nation-building" he had been
promoting. Even so, street demonstrations against his gov
ernment mounted. The United States faced the choice o
aiding the Ky government to stay in power and risk giving
it the label of a puppet government or of letting it fall and
seeking another group of military men to lead South Viet
nam. After so many years of war, the resort to generals a
government heads was inevitable.

No one could doubt that the opposition led by Tri Quang
was adversely affecting the military effort against the Viet
cong, but the troubles seemed to abate after Ky promised
to hold elections.

In the late Spring of 1966, Ambassador Lodge's efforts in
Saigon were directed toward bringing about a reconciliation
between the Buddhists and the Ky regime. But Ky dis
dained conciliation and resorted to the mailed fist against
his rivals. Using tanks and some of his best troops, he offered
them surrender or annihilation and gained the upper hand

At the beginning of June, 1966, there were 260,000 Amer
ican troops in Vietnam. Moreover, almost 2,000 Americans
had been killed in the first five months of the year—com
pared to 1,365 in all of 1965. The fighting was steadily in
tensifying. At the end of June the United States for the firs
time was bombing the oil depots on the outskirts of Hano
and Haiphong. Critics around the world regarded these
attacks as escalation; the President defended them as "th
right course." During the summer the bombings were wid
ened, the targets including not only the oil fields of th
North but also missile sites, power stations, and the demili
tarized zone (DMZ) between the two Vietnams. It was more
over clear that by the end of the year, 400,000 United State
troops would be in South Vietnam.

Meanwhile, South Vietnam held elections in September

110

Their result was a constituent assembly whose task it would be to draft a constitution. The large turnout of voters, reported to be 80.8 percent of the population, was celebrated as a triumph for the Ky regime as well as a tribute to the labors of Ambassador Lodge and his aides in Saigon.

As the United Nations' General Assembly opened in September, the Administration in Washington once more was pressing Hanoi to come to the bargaining table. The President this time offered to de-escalate the war without insisting on solid evidence that North Vietnam also would de-escalate. He was willing to accept "assurances" as sufficient. He also announced that he would go to Manila to attend a meeting of the United States allies in Asia. The President's presence in Asia would give him an opportunity to visit troops in South Vietnam.

At the year's end, in spite of these moves—because they had no success, and quite as if they had never been made, the President was under heavy criticism at home and abroad; public discontent at home was on the rise. Bill Moyers announced that he would leave the White House on January 31 to go into newspaper publishing; George Christian, another Texan, was named to succeed him as Press Secretary. The diplomatic situation was unchanged; neither side gave ground. In his State of the Union Message for 1967, the President spoke of the need for patience and for "staying power." He flew to Guam in March, to meet again with South Vietnamese and American leaders from Saigon. He appeared ready to step up the fighting further in order to bring North Vietnam to the peace table. Yet he simultaneously wrote a letter to Ho Chi Minh, urging the inception of "direct talks" as a way out of the impasse.

As the year 1967 began, the hopes of 1966 for imminent settlement had proved illusory. The United States had added a total of 200,000 troops to the battle and was fairly certain that with almost 400,000 GI's engaged in the struggle, the

111

tide against the Communist forces would begin to turn. I
South Vietnam, the pacification movement continued as th
South Vietnamese army accepted a policy of trying to hol
the populated areas it had won—through "revolutionary d
velopment," that is, civil reform—rather than merely swee
ing through them. In his State of the Union Message th
President declared that in Vietnam "we face more cost, mo
loss, and more agony." But, "we are going to persist—and w
will succeed."

Pressure on the Administration to halt the bombing
North Vietnam increased. In the first week of February, a
unexpected break in the deadlock seemed to be in sight. I
a public broadcast, the North Vietnamese Foreign Minist
Nguyen Duy Trinh declared that there could be talks wit
the United States, but only after "an unconditional halt i
the American bombing." The Administration was told th
this broadcast was a diplomatic signal. Communist and no
Communist intermediaries combined to direct the attentio
of American officials to the significance of Trinh's word
The President revealed his evident eagerness to respon
favorably when on February 2nd he said at his press co
ference that he would order a suspension of the bombing
the North Vietnamese government took "just almost an
step" to justify such a move. Meanwhile, Secretary Rusk l
it be known that the enemy had been informed that th
Vietcong would be accepted at peace talks "as a full negotia
ing party." Both sides now awaited the Tet or Lunar Ne
Year stand-down scheduled for February 8.

When the truce ended on February 11, the United Stat
postponed a resumption of the bombing. Pope Paul V
British Prime Minister Harold Wilson, Secretary-General
Thant—among other world figures—had urged the Unite
States to extend the truce indefinitely. President Johnso
refused to be forced into a unilateral concession. He w
said to fear that if disappointment followed such a mov

he would be under pressure which he might not be able to resist, to escalate the war in the North even further. On finding out that the truce had been used by North Vietnam to resupply its troops, the President felt he could not but resume full-scale bombing.

Late in the Spring of 1967, General Westmoreland was in the United States where he told a joint session of Congress: "We will prevail in Vietnam against the Communist aggressor." That same week, United States bombers struck at the MIG bases in North Vietnam. The war was again growing in scope: 480,000 men were scheduled to be in South Vietnam by the end of the year and there was even talk of half a million. This enlargement of the war called forth fresh opposition, stronger every day.

III.

LAST DAYS BEFORE THE TET OFFENSIVE

BY THE SUMMER OF 1967, THE PROCESS OF "NATION-BUILDING" in South Vietnam had seemingly advanced far enough to permit planning a general election. Lieutenant-General Nguyen Van Thieu, the Chief of State, stood for the Presidency, Nguyen Cao Ky for the Vice-Presidency. The South Vietnamese government pledged itself to insure a fair ballot. Early in August President Johnson formalized to the generals his response to their fresh request for additional troops —for 100,000 more: he would allow them 45,000 and thus bring the strength of the force in Vietnam to about 525,000 by the middle of 1968.

The extent to which the war and the American domestic scene were linked was shown again when the President asked for a ten percent surcharge tax on personal and corporate income, effective October 1. The aim was to help reduce the pressure of inflation in the economy. At the same time, civil disorder in the cities mounted. Passions were aroused by conditions in the urban "ghettos" and many thought poverty could be wiped out if the money being spent on the war were diverted to the home front. The President was reluctant to initiate new programs and waited for a report from his Advisory Commission on Civil Disorders, whose chairman, Governor Otto D. Kerner of Illinois, had a broad mandate to seek the causes of the urban "uprisings."

The President again stated his eagerness to end the bombing of the North. It sprang, he said, from the hope for reciprocal military restraint by the enemy. The President implied that the slowness of "the other side" to respond to *any* conciliatory move was due to the clear encouragement it received from the dissenters in America.

The rising discontent had become a national issue as October, 1967 ended. A group calling itself the National Mobilization to End the War in Vietnam led a mass protest in Washington on October 21. The Administration was torn: should it call a bombing halt to satisfy the growing opposition at home or should it intensify the war in order to satisfy the "hawks"?

On September 3, the people of South Vietnam went to the polls to create an elected government. The two-house legislature that was chosen would share responsibility with the President, General Thieu, and the Vice-President, Marshal Ky. The new officials were sworn in on October 31. Thieu pledged that the door to peace would remain open; but, he added: "I am determined not to accept a surrender." When his cabinet was announced, American officials both in Saigon and in Washington expressed disappointment that no opposition figures had been included.

Meanwhile, before the end of November, the public's confidence in President Johnson's management of the war had dropped, according to the polls, to 23 percent—the lowest yet. Secretary Rusk was bearing the heaviest load of the hostility to the Vietnam policy. In order to address a gathering in a New York hotel, he had to be brought there surreptitiously: outside, demonstrators were clashing with policemen. Senator Eugene McCarthy of Minnesota seemed to offer leadership to the anti-war forces when he indicated a desire to challenge the President in the Presidential primaries. The Administration struck back at these blows by displaying confidence in existing policies and in the outcome. General Westmoreland predicted that the United States could begin to withdraw troops from Vietnam within two years. Just before the month was over, the President announced that Secretary McNamara would leave the Pentagon to become the head of the World Bank. The reasons for this departure of a member of the Tuesday Cabinet were not completely clear to the public.

As the year ended, Johnson was plainly attempting to placate the "doves." One means to this end was to express his willingness to accept Vietcong representatives in discussions of the war at the United Nations. A side-effect of this move was to disrupt the unity between Washington and Saigon: President Thieu faced the necessity of reassuring his military commanders that he at least would make no concessions to the enemy.

President Johnson found an unexpected opportunity to meet with the allied military leaders in Vietnam when he decided to attend in Australia the funeral of one of his most loyal collaborators, Prime Minister Harold Holt, who disappeared tragically while swimming. The President turned the trip into a dramatic display of the influence of the United States in the Pacific as he met with leaders of free Asia. The trip, lasting 120 hours, took the President first to Canberra, then to military installations in Thailand and South Vietnam where he exhorted the troops, then to Rome where at the Vatican he met with Pope Paul VI, and then home just in time for Christmas.

On New Year's Day, the North Vietnamese Foreign Minister Nguyen Duy Trinh declared that when the United States ended the bombing of North Vietnam unconditionally, North Vietnam "will hold talks" with the United States. Trinh, having said a year before that if the bombing stopped, talks "could" take place, Secretary Rusk recognized the latest statement as "a new formulation." He added, "It would be premature for me to brush this aside as purely a propaganda ploy."

Shortly, on January 17, 1968, President Johnson delivered his State of the Union Message. In it he spoke of the morale he found: "Americans are prosperous as men have never been in recorded history. Yet there is in the land a certain restlessness, a questioning." Before the week was over, he announced that the new Secretary of Defense would be his long-time informal adviser, Clark Clifford, widely regarded as a "hawk."

On December 19 and 20, 1967, and January 15 and 20, 1968

MY NEW ROUND OF CONVERSATIONS BEGAN JUST BEFORE Christmas, 1967, when I saw Secretaries McNamara and Rusk and the Chairman of the Joint Chiefs of Staff, General Wheeler. The pregnant visits scheduled with President Johnson and his Special Assistant for National Security Affairs, Walt W. Rostow, which were planned for December, had to be postponed at the last minute because of the President's decision to attend the memorial services for Prime Minister Holt in Melbourne. The President was not free enough to see me until after he had delivered his State of the Union Message in January. A fortuitous result of the postponement was that it provided an opportunity to sample the arguments of the decision-makers in the critical time of an ostensible offer by Hanoi to negotiate.

My first call was at the office of Secretary McNamara, who greeted me graciously as usual. Although it was late in the afternoon, and a slight hoarseness in his voice betrayed that he had a cold, he seemed fresh for talk. Since he was about to leave office I asked him if he would take a retrospective look at the war in Vietnam. His response was direct: It was essential, he thought, to have a thorough critique of the war. He himself had not been able to do as much looking back as he "ultimately wants to or as some should." The critique, he felt, ought to reach back to the late 1940's or even to the Second World War, and should be made by those not connected with the events as he had been.

"When would you say that the war began?" I asked. "It began at different times," he replied, "but more important than that is the question, 'When were there opportunities for choice?' " He pointed out that one such opportunity certainly occurred between February and July, 1965, when the bombing of the North began and the first large-scale dispatch of United States fighting men was made. There were "several Y's in the road," said McNamara, some of them offering "wise alternatives." But he did not think it was "profitable" for him to comment on the choosing of alternatives in decisions in which he had participated. Still, with respect to the choices made in 1965, he added emphatically: "I myself believe we chose the right road." He did not say why.

Knowing that wars—even the most carefully planned large-scale wars—are liable to derailment by the unforeseen, I asked him what surprises there had been for him in the course of the war. He replied politely that it is not appropriate for a public official to admit being surprised. He turned the question around and talked of the surprise to "the other side" caused by the United States' action in 1961 (when our ground strength in Vietnam was increased from 800 to 2,100). "Their surprise may have been the reason for our progress in 1962." Then he returned to the original meaning of my question and said that the deterioration of the people's support for the Saigon government in 1963 "surprised us. . . . We did not know how deep the rot was. . . . That critique of the war will have to be made by those who were not so intimately involved. There are lessons to be learned from the surprises."

At this point we were interrupted by a phone call that he said he would have to take on a more private wire than the one on his desk; he left the office for a couple of minutes. On his return, I pushed our colloquy toward the matter of the ardent and growing opposition to the war. Reminding him that opposition to earlier wars had been polit-

121

ical or ethnic or geographical, I asked, "Do you think the opposition this time is generational?" No, he replied, the great body of youth responds to the traditional appeals; for example, the opposition to the war "has not interfered with motivation in the army." He cited a recent column by Max Lerner in which Lerner wrote he was able to discern three kinds of youth: the suburban, the disadvantaged, and the great middle group. The latter, said McNamara, clearly still responds to the old ideals.

DISSENTING YOUTH

Then, I asked him, why is there such strong opposition to the war on the campuses? "I am not familiar with all the reasons," he replied; but he admitted being troubled by the fact that the opposition was greatest where "the quality of the university is high." On this point he compared the private Eastern universities with the state universities. With an earnest expression he added that at a commencement where he had received an honorary degree the previous year the candidates for the B.A. were seated in four groups corresponding to the levels of honors. The higher the level, the fiercer was the hostility to him as a symbol of the war.

His leg swinging over the arm of the chair, he talked of the opposition without rancor, remarking that the political scientists were less opposed than the physical scientists. His previous point about the quality of the universities came back to him and he hazarded the guess that "possibly there are more physical scientists in good schools." Clearly, he said, it was ground for concern that young intellectuals feel unable to support the war and that they have "a different set of objectives." Because there was always a ten-year lag between the politics of the nation and the ideas of its intellectuals, "it worries me to think about the future. . . .

The gap breeds weakness in national policy," he pointed out with some despondency.

In the future that McNamara had in mind, I readily drew from him that China would be a determinative force—an "unsettling, de-stabilizing influence." She is "not necessarily going to commit major military aggression," but she will project beyond her borders and become a threat to the whole world.

One of the reasons that he looked forward to going to the World Bank,* he went on pensively, was that the Bank helps deal with the enormous problems arising in many parts of the world because of population growth in the face of "unacceptably low food production." Large scale privation, he said, "breeds weakness that China can take advantage of," and, he added, "it translates back to restrictions on political liberties."

I then turned his thoughts to the irony that many people who only recently had been denouncing the war in Vietnam as "McNamara's War" were now deploring his forthcoming departure from the Defense Department as a defeat for the "doves"—who had found encouragement for their views in some of his recent public utterances. Here McNamara began to speak fervently, saying that his position was being misunderstood. He compared his stand on the war with Senator Eugene McCarthy's which he described as "soft, mentally and politically." When McCarthy talks about improving the military position of the United States through withdrawal, McNamara said, he "talks nonsense." As for himself, McNamara explained, when he opposed the bombing of Phuc Yen, he did so "because it's contrary to the national interest, and I think I can prove it." ** "McCarthy and I," he con-

* He took over early in 1968.
** Phuc Yen is a town containing an airstrip, 17 miles NNW of Hanoi. During the weeks when the Trinh statement was being probed, Ameri-

cluded, "have two entirely different approaches to the problem."

My next question followed naturally upon this statement that his position was misunderstood. "Why is there so little articulate support on Capitol Hill for the Administration policies?" He pointed out that some voices were making themselves heard, such as Senator Gale McGee's (Democrat, Wyoming). Still he seemed to agree with my generalization as he said that understanding the why and what of the war involved understanding "quite a subtle position." And he observed that it was "tough to get people to die for something other than unconditional surrender."

The war, he went on, represented "a change from the past." It was a case of "limited objectives being sought by limited means." The value of restraint "has not been discussed enough." Then, as if to give the whole explanation in a word, he said forcefully, "No one can win a nuclear war." Some members of Congress, he thought, had not been exposed to the new military-political theory on which the kind of war we were fighting in Vietnam was based and "thus are still groping for a full understanding of it." "Mel Laird * understands it," he remarked, adding that it was theory going against the military strategy of all the past centuries.

As we broke off because he had to go to a meeting, we exchanged holiday greetings and on my expressing regret that this was the last time we would be talking, he invited me to call on him at the World Bank.

The following morning I was back in the Pentagon, this time for a conversation with General Wheeler. I was agreeably surprised to be met by Colonel Phelps Jones, the Gen-

---

can bombing of the immediate vicinity of Hanoi and Haiphong had been limited lest it jeopardize whatever possibility existed that North Vietnam was shifting its position.

* Representative Melvin R. Laird (Republican, Wisconsin), the ranking member of his party on the House Defense Appropriations Sub-committee; President Nixon appointed him to be Secretary of Defense.

eral's aide for public affairs. I had not seen Jones in a number of years—since he was on the faculty of the United States Military Academy at West Point and I was a guest lecturer there. Shortly, General Wheeler invited me into his office. His desk, one noticed immediately, faced a large map of Vietnam that proclaimed his chief concern. We sat comfortably around a coffee table at the other end of the office, the General lit his pipe and we began to talk.

Upon asking him who in the armed forces played the role of "devil's advocate" regarding established policy, he explained that there were several sources of contrary views. When the Joint Staff prepare papers for the meetings of the Joint Chiefs of Staff—which he told me took place on Monday, Wednesday, and Friday afternoons—they "list the advantages and disadvantages of different courses of action. The process of seeing the pros and cons constitutes the role of devil's advocate." He went on: "My staff group does a separate review of all Joint Chiefs' papers before being read by me." The Joint Chiefs themselves, he said, "suggest betterment or advocate different courses of action" respecting responses to problems brought before them.

He said firmly of the work of the Chiefs: "We examine all aspects of problems ourselves with this criterion in mind: 'If I were the President of the United States, would I approve the course of action being recommended to me by the Joint Chiefs?'" Wheeler also said that the Chiefs took into account political, social, and psychological factors as well as those purely military, "these considerations having been enjoined upon the Chiefs by several Presidents."

We went on to the problem of opposition to the war and the consequences thereof for its conduct. "Does it become a factor in making decisions?" I asked. "Not directly," he replied. "The Chiefs are well aware of the problems engendered for the President by the minority dissent to his course of action," but the Chiefs have never "changed substantially" a recommendation of theirs on that account. "The national security interest" of the United States is the issue, and "while the opposition must be recognized and countered it does not sway us from what we recommend."

"A facet of the opposition's argument," he pointed out, "was that the air attacks on North Vietnam were indiscriminate. That was not so." He stated, "A great deal of attention is given to assuring that operations are mounted in such a way as to minimize civil damage." The Joint Chiefs, he said, "have never advocated attacking the dikes in order to flood the Red River delta or using the populace as a target. . . . I know that the opposite view is a facet of the young people's position." "Contrary to Herblock* and others, the aim is not to kill people," he avowed. "To follow any other policy would put a club in the hands of the dissenters."

I asked the General why he thought young people were so numerous among the dissenters. "Some of these youngsters," he said in a bland tone, "are just misled by their elders." He went on, "I question the motives of the leaders of the dissent. They are not opposed to war as such; they are not Quakers; they are not honest-to-God dissenters." The leaders know "exactly what they are doing," he said, and as a result many young people are innocently following the Hanoi line. Wheeler, describing the situation as "regrettable," had a tone of sadness in his voice, not anger.

I asked Wheeler as I had asked McNamara what surprises, if any, he had experienced as the war unfolded. He seemed keen to answer. In late 1963, he said, he had gone to Saigon for President Kennedy to survey the Vietnam situation. "I came away certain that we were on the right course of action militarily." He thought then that only logistical and support help would be required. "I believed that the war was progressing well and that success for the ARVN [South Vietnam's army] was predictable. I had no qualms in my

* The syndicated cartoonist, Herbert L. Block.

own mind," he continued. Then "the Mad Monk, Tri Quang, began his activities in the American press, which began to talk about a solidly Buddhist country—even though there are twenty-six distinct ethnic and religious groups there. The government gave us a mighty surprise when it could not handle the resulting turmoil. The government proved feckless, and successive governments were increasingly worthless and ineffectual."

Still, the armed forces of South Vietnam did not fall apart. Why not? He put the question himself as he went on in the manner of a briefing officer. "In 1964 I brought back the answer from Vietnam. We had inserted advisers at all unit levels down to and including battalions. They were like the steel reinforcing rods in concrete."

This reinforcement was adequate until the beginning of 1965 when the ARVN began to fail. "The senior officers were in politics rather than in the war effort." What surprised him, he said, was that the ARVN remained cohesive as long as it did. In an afterthought, he remarked that Ky and Thieu "with a less effective government had put Tri Quang out of business." It has "always puzzled me" that their predecessor governments had not been able to do this. Through it all, under Generals Harkins and Westmoreland, "the concrete held together." Then the North Vietnamese began to introduce regular army units, and "since then there have been no surprises of any consequence."

The subject of surprises led him naturally to the performance of American men in the field. Some people had predicted, he said, "that between the climate and the guerrillas the American troops could not survive." Skeptics had forgotten that American soldiers had fought "the best guerrillas, the Plains Indians, for a hundred years. We have yet to see or read about better guerrillas than those were. Moreover, Americans had battled against guerrillas in the Second World War, too, and he mentioned the struggle in New Guinea. A pleasant surprise, he added, was that "in the middle of a war for survival" South Vietnam had been able "to hold elections and establish a government that includes a Constituent Assembly, a President, and a Supreme Court."

AN ENCLAVE STRATEGY

Looking toward future events, I asked General Wheeler if he could foresee the United States taking a military position that might be "somewhere between escalation and withdrawal." He smiled and asked whether I was talking about the enclave idea. I said "yes" and he began to deal with it. "Unless you match or overmatch the action taken by the enemy," he said, "predictably you're going to lose. . . . The side with the initiative comes out on top. If you lose the initiative, you'll lose the military success you are seeking. . . . Field commanders throughout history have broken their backs to achieve the initiative. You must carry the fight to the enemy." And, in soldier's language, he said: "No one ever won a battle sitting on his ass."

He expatiated: to dig in in enclaves enables the enemy to move at will and feed himself. The battle of Dien Bien Phu, he declared, was a perfect example. "The French smacked themselves down with mountains around them. They had created an enclave, and the consequences were predictable: the enemy could choose its time and place."

I used the word "escalation" again, whereupon Wheeler stopped to tell me that it is not a good military term. "We don't use it as the newspapers do. We use it in the sense of going from one type of war to another, from conventional to nuclear. Escalation cannot occur within the parameters set by the President."

We talked again about the opposition to the war, which led Wheeler to use the word "irresponsible" about some of the utterances of dissent. He said: "It's hard to get the other side [meaning this time the domestic opponents] to stop talking long enough to listen. It's hard to get through the wall of words they throw up around themselves." But, he declared philosophically, "I'm old enough not to be contentious."

I wondered what he thought were the underlying reasons for the opposition to the war. Wheeler responded with neo-isolationism. "These parishioners get into the church by different doors. . . . I am not questioning their motives," he added, though "some of their motives are not clear. Many of these critics are sincerely worried that we have too many commitments to other people." They ask, "What happens if all these due notes are called in a relatively short time? . . . Another group is worried about the financial position of the country." They cite the cost of NATO as an example. "Others feel that the NATO nations have not done enough to defend themselves." Still another group believes that the expenditure of money abroad "lessens the sums available at home." They say "first things first," and "charity begins at home."

And then domestic politics is involved, too. Some of "the struggle or contention is reflected in attitudes toward the war itself." I suggested that racism might be a factor, although I myself had not observed it. I was thinking of the idea President Johnson had expressed, that aid in defense of freedom to people of color, such as the Vietnamese, was less popular than aid for the same purpose to white people, such as the peoples of Europe. "I think this is true," said Wheeler; and finally, "some think that Administration policy is not in the best interest of the United States national security interest." I asked Wheeler what he thought of General Shoup's recent sharp criticism of Administration policy.* "No member of the Joint Chiefs agrees with Shoup at all," was his instantaneous reply.

* David M. Shoup, who had been Commandant of the United States Marine Corps, 1960–1963, had denounced the President's contention that the Vietnam War was vital to United States interests as "pure un-

"Tell me, General," I now asked, "to what extent is the war in Vietnam a civil war?" He replied like a man who had thought about the problem: "There is," he said, "a civil war aspect to it." He instanced a dissident group "ethnically South Vietnamese," that was taken north as part of the original apparatus for a take-over. "We know that Hanoi is plotting directly and supporting this element at different levels of violence. But the level of violence was gradually raised until it turned the struggle into a typical conventional war."

"Is the enemy in the south all Communist?" I asked. "I don't think so," he replied, "but the Communists are in basic control. The whole thrust comes from Hanoi. The Communist party in the south is a branch of the Lao Dong Party [the Communist party of North Vietnam]."

But, he concluded, this was not a civil war in the sense of the kind of civil war we in the United States fought. "We had two groups (a third if you count Copperheads and whatnot) that were opposed on the question of basic structure. But they were not directed from outside. In Vietnam the aggression is from the outside—'a war of national liberation,' an external war." he said firmly. "We have sensitive sources of information," he added, in authentication of his remarks.

At this point, I shifted the conversation to a matter long of interest to me, and did it (I now fear) much too bluntly. I wanted to know how good was the technological help that North Vietnam was receiving from its friends? The North Vietnamese, he replied, were receiving such assistance as they were capable of using. "North Vietnam does not have a broad base of technicians. He described the Soviet materiel— MIG's, surface-to-air missiles, and radar equipment, as "sophisticated and good." In talking of aid from the U.S.S.R.

---

adulterated poppycock," maintaining that the struggle was a civil war (*The New York Times,* Dec. 17, 1967).

and the fact that the Soviets had not supplied surface-to-surface missiles, he expressed the opinion that the Soviet Union did not want a confrontation with the United States in any circumstances—"certainly not over North Vietnam. . . . I can imagine what would happen in the United States if a Soviet missile hit a United States destroyer the way the *Elath* [the Israeli destroyer] was hit off Port Said." "Of course," he said more deliberately, "I could be proved a pretty poor prophet." But his firm conviction was that the Soviets would not give the North Vietnamese such a military capability.

Looking next at China's role in helping the North Vietnamese, Wheeler said, "The CHICOMS [Pentagonese for Chinese Communists] are doing three things: they are providing logistical support, particularly smaller weapons, ammunition, and hand grenades. They are supplying engineer units in the northern part of North Vietnam to repair what we knock down. They are helping to man the anti-aircraft weapons." He added, "We think that there are technical advisers present, too, but the number is not so substantial that we can confirm this." Then Wheeler summed up: "I do not believe that the CHICOMS honestly believe we have any intention of attacking China."

I turned the talk to a subject that historians may one day ponder: the war in Vietnam was the first American war that did not seem to generate public heroes. Wheeler did not doubt the validity of that judgment. Of course, he said, the pros knew that this was more of a "professional's war" than any in the past. "It's not the kind of war that lends itself to glamour," and by way of comparison he mentioned a few great moments in the Second World War, including the breakout at St. Lô and the piercing of the Siegfried Line. Pointing out the absence of tank warfare in Vietnam, he suggested the notion that a war of movement was in itself dramatic. Then he said, with a smile: "There were no heroes in the Indian wars either—only one in reverse: General Custer."

He added another reason, prefacing his words with an apology for their being an "unkind remark": "No war has ever been the subject of so damned much uninformed comment. I am appalled sometimes by what I read." Of course, he said immediately, "I have my own point of view." This brought his mind back to the difference between this war and others in the past. "It is not a war of front lines. In World War II you could measure progress on situation maps. The Germans ran out of ground to stand on. The problem in Vietnam is to gain control of people; the terrain is not that valuable; there are many uninhabited portions."

I wanted to hear more from Wheeler on the way the war was being reported to the public: "Are the so-called media responsible for what you criticize?" He said, "The media frequently write about the wrong things because they are searching for a headline." He cited as examples the pictures of the wounded and those showing fires being set to thatched huts. These huts, he declared, were usually enemy bunkers. A result of showing such lurid scenes, was to make General Westmoreland seem "like Attila returned in a second incarnation. . . . I'll be damned if I know how to set it aright," he said resignedly. "Maybe we need a hero."

Wheeler had been the army officer selected to brief President Kennedy on military affairs after the election in 1960. The sessions with Kennedy had helped pave the way for Wheeler's appointment as Army Chief of Staff. I remember thinking of that as I left the Pentagon, and understanding better the appeal he had to the civilian leaders.

The same afternoon I went to visit Secretary Rusk. He greeted me somewhat distractedly, I thought. As I sat down I remarked that it was almost two years since I had last spoken with him, and this made my first question obvious: "What changes in the war have occurred in the past two

132

years?" Without hesitation Rusk answered: "Military defeat is now excluded; only a small fraction of the power available in Vietnam can even be used." He talked of the "countable indicators" that showed the progress being made: the rise in the enemy's rate of defection, the drop in recruitment by the Vietcong in the South, the drop in the number of desertions from government forces, the drop in the number of arms lost as compared to arms captured, the casualty rates, the number of roads opened.

Having just returned from a meeting of the NATO ministers, he said he could state confidently that the war in Vietnam was not a stumbling block to international discussions. Of the ninety-five diplomats he met in Brussels at the NATO meeting, he said, only three or four mentioned the subject of the war, and he had not even received an *aide-memoire* on the subject in six months. He asked rhetorically: "What does this reflect? The Allied countries wish the war would disappear but they recognize that the attitude of the United States under a security treaty is of some importance to them." The Asian nations, he then added, felt very strongly about this, too.

I asked him how the political side of the war was going. He promptly referred—as Wheeler had—to the elections in South Vietnam and the government created there in the midst of war as constituting something "close to a miracle." Remember, he said, that a "tough, pervasive guerrilla force" which was preaching "if you vote, you die" could not prevent a turnout of between sixty and seventy percent of the voters. He went on: "People don't think or worry about coups any more." Besides, he said, there is "movement on the economic front: runaway inflation has been stemmed." At the same time, "We'd like to see pacification and rural development move faster."

As with McNamara and Wheeler, I was eager to have his views on the opposition to the war. His voice in reply sugested barely suppressed anger. He told how 17,000 students at Indiana University had signed a statement of apology for the heckling he had received from a handful of dissenting students there, but that the dissenters had received the attention from the press, and the apology had not. "Three students with a sign on a campus can get equal time with me on television." He continued, commenting next that the hippies must be measured against the three million young people who are in uniform. "Youth, in general, are not significantly different from the rest of the population."

I asked Rusk to explain what, in his own view, makes this opposition so effective: "The Communist apparatus is working all around the world." But immediately he added the caution that one must avoid the smear technique; it could produce "a new wave of McCarthyism." He could understand "dedicated conscientious pacifists like the Quakers"—by which he implied but did not say that he could not understand other dissenters. He described, though, how their arguments ran: "Vietnam is too far away. Treaties are not that important. Ho could be made into Tito. All those fighting out there are Vietnamese; therefore let them figure it out for themselves." Some of the opposition, he wound up, is "of course, just plain political."

He was sure that opposition to the war was not peculiar to any single age-group in the population. "More than twenty years have passed since World War II. There is an inclination to forget a great deal. Some forget or get careless. Others have had no chance to remember." In this connection he noted that the average college student "was in the sixth grade when I became Secretary of State." As the Second World War recedes into the past, the recollection of "the price paid to write Article I of the UN Charter [aimed at preventing aggression] is also slipping into the background. . . . Few people read that article, which drew together the lessons of experience of my generation. It is the only guide we have to prevent World War III." He added solemnly, "There will be no chance to learn from World War III."

Coming back once more to the importance of the passage of time, he said: "It makes difficult some central issues we were conversant with in 1945. It makes it too easy in the 1960's to drift back into a false comfort." He listed Manchuria, Ethiopia, the Rhineland, Austria, and spoke of the general attitude toward Hitler at first; it had been: "Give him another bite; he doesn't really mean it." Rusk mentioned *Mein Kampf* and equated with it "the doctrine spewing out of Peking."

"Why," I asked, "is the support of Administration policy so little vocal?" Rusk shot back: "What is news, McGee or Fulbright? Who gets the attention? . . . Two thousand stories could be filed. If a sergeant gets into a brawl in a bar, it is reported; but 1999 acts of kindness and cooperation are not reported." He returned to his own efforts: "It is not easy to repeat myself and get it printed." And to broaden the point he added: "This is the first struggle that has been fought on television."

REVIVED ISOLATIONISM

Then he pondered the continued vitality of isolationism as a national phenomenon, and, more specifically, the new isolationist view that Asia was an unimportant part of the world. "Scratch the skin of any American and you find he wants to take care of his own affairs and not get involved. . . . There is no *imperium* in Americans—at least not in the post-war period. . . . Acts of will since World War II have not erased the institution of isolationism." Perhaps, he summed up, "it is a feeling in most people in most places.

"The alternative to meeting one's commitments," Rusk said sternly, "is isolation. They cannot be met selectively."

"There is nothing more serious than a treaty commitment," he said. Then he spoke as he had done once before of President Kennedy's confrontation with Premier Khrushchev in Vienna. When Kennedy said to Khrushchev, "Don't kid me," declared Rusk, "the President *had* to be believed—as he had to be believed during the Cuban missile crisis. Hundreds of millions of lives were at stake." Rusk concluded: "The issue being tested in Vietnam is credibility." A few minutes later in further clarifying what he saw at stake, Rusk added: "The civil war idea will not stand up; some elements of a civil war are present. There are authentic dissidents in the South; but there is also aggression from North Vietnam. Those combat troops are not there [in South Vietnam] because of what the indigenous Southern dissidents are doing."

Then he moved abruptly to the Administration's proposal for halting the war: "We say, 'Put on the table a schedule of what you'll withdraw; and we will do the same.'" He clinched the point: "If what the North is doing would stop, the South could work things out." He went on to note that no one was alleging that the German problem was a problem of a civil war. Similarly, "Korea was not a civil war. In Vietnam the issue is the same one of aggression as in cases of national frontiers that are well established. Aggression is at the heart of the issue."

I asked Rusk, "Who now plays the role of devil's advocate that George Ball was once supposed to have played?" * Rusk said Ball had only played that role when he was "assigned" it. Then, "there is a constant boxing of the compass in these matters. A decision only means choosing among alternatives," and—he was emphatic—no ideas have come from outside the Department of State that have not been thought

* Ball had resigned as Undersecretary of State in 1966; he returned to the Administration as United States Ambassador to the United Nations, succeeding Arthur Goldberg in April, 1968.

of and discussed inside it. In fact "we have discussed some ideas that have not gotten into print yet." Before I could ask him what these were he said with a grin that he was not going to say what they were.

"If no alternatives are proposed," said Rusk, "the President will call them forward. . . . He will sometimes go around the table to see that this is being done. . . . The President won't permit himself to be shielded from opposing points of view." Moreover, according to Rusk, the President "follows what is said publicly in newspapers and resolutions and he sees 85 chiefs of government." Rusk listed as evidence of the President's contacts with the rest of the world his visit to Expo '67, his trip to Manila, his participation in the Punta del Este Conference, and his journey to the Adenauer funeral.

I asked Rusk as I had asked his colleagues: "Have you had surprises about the way the war has gone on?" He answered: "I'd rather not talk about surprises. If anyone had asked me three years ago whether we could have 500,000 men there and bomb as we have, without bringing in the Chinese, I would have had to say no."

I wanted to keep him on the subject of China which I could see was deemed by the Administration central to all foreign policy decisions. The Secretary pressed on me the fact that China was not being forced into "an orgasm of decision-making"—a phrase he had used previously in our conversations—because we have "geared our responses to the other side and have kept open the possibility of deescalating." Still, he repeated what he had said, he was "surprised at Big Brother's attitude."

"What about the role of the Soviet Union in the Vietnam War?" I asked. "We can recognize their interest in North Vietnam. . . . Their response had been about what was expected." He said he believes that there was now a better balance in Hanoi between the influence of Moscow and the influence of Peking. I interjected that the last time we talked he had told me that Peking controlled Hanoi. He responded: "Hanoi could decide to call this thing off in a way it could not do two years ago." He remained certain, though, as he was the last time, that "when it ends it will end rather suddenly."

Then, with an air of satisfaction somewhat unconvincing, he said, "The work of the world goes on despite Vietnam. It has not infected the total of diplomacy; it hasn't stopped everything else in its tracks." He listed activities and achievements in other fields, including the International Monetary Fund, the nuclear non-proliferation treaty, the Civil Air Agreement, the Asian Development Bank, and the progress in the Middle East and on Cyprus.

Referring now to the possibilities for peace, I asked him if the South Vietnamese government could make a settlement with "the other side" separately from America's settlement. Yes, he replied, "if the other side wanted to break this thing up into pieces they can. The part of it which is an authentic civil war can be settled in the South. We would not consider that to be a major departure in policy." On the subject of recognizing the Vietcong, he sallied: "Recognize them as what? They do not claim to be a government. Recognize them as a body fighting? We do that: we shoot at 'em every day." As to a halt in the bombing that would be "permanent and unconditional," he was adamant. That phrase, he said, "was imprecise. . . . we *have* to be precise."

As our meeting ended, I asked Rusk when he was going to come back to Scarsdale, his home community and mine. He could not say, but when he did, he said, he will be "broke and unemployed." Was he still determined not to write his memoirs? "Yes," he would never write a "now-it-can-be-told" book. When I left he was about to receive a delegation of Thais; they were waiting in the reception room.

Three weeks later I was again in the White House. The

President's round-the-world journey and his stay at the LBJ Ranch during the holidays had intervened. But it was Walt Rostow I had come to visit, the President's Special Assistant for National Security Affairs. His office was in the basement of the West Wing. Rostow, a voluble man like his predecessor McGeorge Bundy, had an ingratiating manner. As I entered his office and we shook hands, he said to me casually, "Have a grape." He pinched one off for himself from a bunch in a bowl of fruit. When we had settled down on his sofa, I asked him if he would put on his old hat as an historian and regard my questions as the kind that historians wish had been answered by the leaders of other wartime administrations. He said he was fascinated by the idea, promising to be as frank with me as he was with his wife, another well-known historian.

I began: "Has there been a change in the international weather in the last month, making the period an historic turning point in the war?" I was referring to the Trinh statement, as he knew.* He replied simply, "A question mark has arisen." Trinh's words, he said, were compatible with the San Antonio formula,** which he described as "rock bottom; just not negotiable." The Administration was exerting every effort to determine the full meaning of the Trinh statement. "You gotta know when you don't know." Would he tell me how these efforts were being undertaken? "Not one word," was his answer. Then he volunteered, when I asked him what the expectations were: "McNamara sees no chance; Rusk keeps a glimmer. I think there's a ten percent possibility that we can end the war in the next six

* See p. 119.
** President Johnson's offer "to stop all aerial and naval bombardment of North Vietnam when this will lead promptly to productive discussions." It was contained in an address delivered before the National Legislative Conference on September 29, 1967. *Public Papers of the Presidents of the United States: Lyndon B. Johnson, 1967,* Book II (Washington, 1968), p. 879.

months." He inserted as an afterthought: "But you can't get caught in a phony offer."

Then we talked about the course of the war. General Westmoreland's statement of the previous year that the number of American troops in Vietnam could be reduced in two years was "the outer limit of optimism," he said. "As a government we are not locked into this position and we are working on a long-term horizon." Maybe, he added, there would be "a change after the 1968 election—if no Mendès is elected." * The Asian leaders who gathered in Melbourne, he pointed out, were saying to President Johnson, "Get elected and they'll talk [meaning the enemy]." The question is, Rostow went on, "Are 'they' coming to the same judgment as we are about the war?" He declared that since the fourth quarter of 1966, the war had been running in a way "bound to produce a cave-in." The other side, in the period from 1964 to 1966, he said, was trying to win by "a modified Mao third-stage offensive." They were on their way to winning "until United States troops entered." There will be no "protracted war," he said confidently.

ENEMY STRENGTH

Rostow talked of how the base of Vietcong manpower was being eroded. "The clock is ticking on them," he began. In 1967, "with the extension of security in the countryside," a million and a half more people came under the control of the Saigon government, he said. The drifting away of the population from Vietcong control was being aided, he went on, by a general pull toward the cities, which were safe, and where wages were higher owing to the construction boom produced by the presence of the United States. As far as

* The allusion was to Pierre Mendès-France, who, as French premier in the early 1950's, helped to disengage France from its involvement in Indochina.

140

nation-building was concerned, he asserted, "in many ways what the South Vietnamese have done in the last few years is miraculous."

Militarily, Rostow said, the Vietcong confront "waning possibilities in the field." They were shifting the burden of the fighting to the frontiers—toward the DMZ and toward Laos and Cambodia—in order to reduce the pressure on the Vietcong structure and to provide a substitute for the bases they had lost in the Iron Triangle.* He spoke also of how North Vietnamese troops were increasingly being used as "filler" in the Vietcong units. Overall in the country they represented ten percent of the troops, he estimated, and twenty percent in I Corps.** The Vietcong "should not be strapped for manpower," he said, but the bombing "has put a strain on them. They are measuring the weight of their losses against the loss of support for President Johnson in the United States. . . . Time is no longer their friend politically in the United States."

We began then to talk about the effects of the bombing on the war as a whole. For one thing, Rostow said, "I smell but have no solid information that Soviet influence [in Hanoi] may be marginally greater." He explained that the bombing had so raised the aid bill that the Soviet Union as the supplier of 80 percent of the aid probably had gained "more leverage." He described China as "a great dragon with a bellyache," a country with "a lot of troubles" and, therefore, less able to help. The United States was trying to organize the defense of Asia because of China, he went on. The Soviets wanted the Americans to go home because they calculated that the Americans, by their presence in that part of the world, were "pricking up the goddam Chinks"—words

---

* A major Vietcong base area, northwest of Saigon on the Saigon River.
** Articulated as "eye-core" in army pronunciation, it was the first, and northernmost, of the four corps areas, or military zones, into which South Vietnam had been divided.

he used in order to suggest how he imagined the Soviet leaders talked about the problem in their inner councils.

We discussed the kinds of equipment that were being supplied by the Soviets and he said that the Soviets were using the war as a proving ground. I asked why he thought the Soviets had not supplied North Vietnam with surface-to-surface missiles. He answered, "*We* are exercising restraint." If they were used, "it is possible that we might go into a 'Cuban' missile crisis." He said that the Mark II missile was there but not the Mark III, "which the Israelis say is in Egypt." The air defense system around Hanoi, he said, was "the most sophisticated anywhere in the world," but the American pilots have turned in a "very great performance. . . . We use special weapons so as not to kill civilians."

Continuing, Rostow observed that the purpose of bombing "was not like [that in] World War II." Rather, "it is an economical way to impose an awkward inconvenience. Hanoi must run its economy and logistical system at a lower throttle." He said that the bombing was tying down some of Hanoi's "best manpower"—its more highly-trained people. He estimated that 700,000 people were being immobilized in this fashion, which, he pointed out, was about equal in number to the Vietcong, and thus presumably a counterweight on the scale. "Can we increase the burden on the North?" I asked. He replied, "At the present stage this is the maximum you can impose on them."

"Would the bombing of Haiphong make a difference?" He said the question called for "a complicated calculus." It would not, he said, stop the flow of imports but simply divert it to less adequate ports or to land routes from China. He did not think the mining of Haiphong's harbor could be decisive. Such a step might in fact put Hanoi "more in the hands of China." He said, "Even now, the North is not really able to control the throttle, because it is dependent on outside help." We were on the subject of China again. China, he said, was using its influence to keep things going, but "wouldn't object if Hanoi wanted to get out."

I now took up the opposition to the war. What, I asked my fellow-historian, does this dissent rest on? Supporting our actions in Vietnam, he said, "is like backing the police. . . . It's hard to get the bands out. Yet you've got to have law and order." People know that "despite its obscurities" the war is necessary in order to avoid a "bigger and more unpleasant one later. . . . The consequences of pulling out would be something worse." Anyhow, "the nation is not in a bug-out mood. . . . History will salute us," he said with certainty.

I was about to broach another subject when the phone rang. Rostow said briskly: "That's the President." He picked up the phone and said with great deference, "Hello, good morning, sir," just as I stepped out of the office to give him privacy.

The call finished, I was back inside. "Have you been surprised by any of the events in the Vietnam War?" I asked. "Yes," he responded intensely, "we were terrorized by the depth of the erosion in South Vietnam in 1961. The situation could only be retrieved convulsively. By 1965, we knew where we were." "Any surprises since then?" I asked. His answer was: "The world has accepted better than expected the bombing of North Vietnam." On the other hand, there were pleasant surprises, too. He mentioned how the American troops were put into combat, had to "learn the name of the game," and "were not kicked around."

Rostow wanted me to be aware of the importance of the things aside from Vietnam that were taking the President's energy in the field of foreign affairs. Down at the Ranch after his operation, the President saw that what he might be able to achieve in office "hinged on what he did elsewhere in the world than Vietnam." Behind the shield of the Vietnam thing, said Rostow, the President hoped to build a new order in Asia and other parts of the world.

Rostow thereupon developed what was, in essence, the thesis of his lectures at the University of Leeds the previous February,* namely, that the United States having filled the power vacuum after the Second World War, was seeking to fall back all over the world from "overbearing, bilateral relationships" and accepting "junior partnerships." But he made an exception: "the nuclear thing." There was, he said, "no escaping United States nuclear responsibilities." In mentioning the nuclear non-proliferation treaty, he spoke soberly about the obligation of the United States to protect others. America, he said, would not be able to avoid "carrying the can for others on nuclear blackmail."

We talked a little longer and then because Rostow had to go to a meeting we broke off. I went to Capitol Hill. Senator Claiborne Pell of Rhode Island, with whom I serve on the National Historical Publications Commission, had invited me to have lunch with him when we met by chance at Union Station and shared a taxi into town the night before. A member of the Senate Committee on Foreign Relations, he was a "de-escalator," as was Senator Frank Church of Idaho, a fellow Democrat on the Committee, to whom he introduced me as we ate in the Senate Dining Room. Across the room sat Senator Morse and his luncheon guests. How much more than the single mile measured on the ground separated the Executive Branch from this part of the Legislative Branch! I mused about this as the meal progressed and Pell and I talked about the war. We discussed the Administration's arguments and Pell's experiences in talking to North Vietnam spokesmen—Mai Van Bo particularly—in 1967 in Paris. I took no notes, but I remembered well Pell's casual comment even as he criti-

* Published in 1967 by the Leeds University Press, under the title *The Great Transition: Tasks of the First and Second Post-War Generations.*

cized the President's war policies: "Johnson must have an I.Q. of 200."

The President was unable to see me in the early evening as planned because, I was told, he was still at work on his State of the Union Message. After he had delivered it before Congress later in the week the appointment was rescheduled for Saturday. Arriving at the White House a little early, I fell into conversation with Governor Otto Kerner. He told me that the Commission on Civil Disorders he headed was going to issue "a very strong report." He, too, was waiting to see the President—about the other war, the one in the streets. Kerner went into the Oval Office ahead of me and I was escorted to the Fish Room where I waited only a few minutes because Kerner's business turned out to be brief.

When I walked in, the President was standing and reading a memorandum. Looking up, he came toward me, telling me he was glad to see me again, shook hands warmly, and motioned me to sit down. He took his place in his rocker.

I asked him if his trip around the world and the Trinh "peace feeler"—or whatever it was—from Hanoi would make the turn from the old year to the new a significant event in the war's history. "Could be," he replied. "We don't know yet what the significance of their statement is." He clearly wanted to talk about his trip to Australia and Asia, because, he said, its importance had not been recognized sufficiently. "What we did is overlooked by the working press which is generally sensational and superficial."

The President's thoughts were on Australia, especially, a small country "which has done a very great job and which could become another Southwest. I believe basically that might does not make right. Therefore, you don't have to have the greatest fleet like Britain's or an army like Germany's or an air force like ours or a population like China's to exercise influence in the world." The people of Australia, he said, "have frontier attitudes, sound judgment, and courage." In the last war, he declared, he had been stationed there, so he knew about these qualities at first hand. He recalled how the Australians "had stood their ground when the Japanese invaded New Guinea."

THE NEW ASIA

What took him to Australia was his affection for Prime Minister Holt and a regard for the role he had played in helping create the "new Asia." He described how Holt had cooperated with him "in trying to bring together a new regionalism for Asians led by Asians. There was no white superiority in Holt. I asked him to go into the brown countries." The President spoke with enthusiasm and vigor. And, he wanted to make clear: "Holt was not a stooge of the United States."

"I am not a sentimentalist, but Holt looking down from Heaven expected me to be there," he said with feeling about the memorial rites for the Prime Minister. "Poor Holt," he added gloomily, "was eaten by a shark." Because the President's own schedule and the coincidence of the Christmas season left few dates available for the trip to Australia, the Australian government had cooperated by holding the rites on a day convenient to him.

His going to Australia, he said, had "brought Prime Minister Wilson up from his vacation" and it brought all the leaders of free Asia, too. "Every damn one of them was there." He listed the countries they came from: the Republic of China, Korea, Malaysia, the Philippines, Thailand, and he spoke of their leaders by name. "They all sat down at the table with this white man," he said with evident satisfaction.

The President had an aide, James R. Jones, bring me a

146

handsome color photograph taken in the cathedral in Melbourne showing the President at one end of a pew and Wilson at the other end. Between them were the leaders he had been talking about—all of them men of color, and representing, as the President pointed out, "a population ten times that of Australia. . . . They speak with power and authority. He mused: "We showed by our presence that we are together in sorrow as well as sunshine." The President said he had talked with the Asian leaders about the future of their countries. At the Kennedy and Adenauer funerals, Mr. Johnson recalled, "each one wanted to talk to the President of the United States." They know, he said, that the choice "to live or die" is between the new Asia and Communist Asia, "planned right out of Peking."

He moved the focus of the discourse to President Thieu. The press had tried to say that there were differences between him and Thieu regarding peace proposals. But that is "a bunch of fraud, cooked up by the picayunish little phonies. . . . Thieu came in and I talked to him. We tried to evolve some basis of understanding."

The President said he was ready for a peace meeting anywhere. It could include Communist China, the Soviets, Britain, South Vietnam, the United States, North Vietnam, and they could talk to both North Vietnam and South Vietnam. *"The New York Times,"* he said scornfully, "is protecting us from everybody. . . . Our meeting was not a summit conference. The resume made it clear."

The President was sensitive to the charge that the trip to Australia was turned into a public display. "No one in Australia," said this, he declared. They merely ask, "Goddam it, how does he feel about us? . . . They see I traveled 12,000 miles to be there. I won't run out on the people of this country. I won't run out on the people of South Vietnam. The truth is, I'm not going to sell out anyone."

Then he discussed his trip to Rome. The Pope, he said,

147

wanted some information. "It was just as close to come back by Rome." The President spoke of how the fact of his intention to visit the Pope had leaked out and helped the Communists in Italy organize demonstrations. "It could not have been leaked except by the Secretary of State. He told an assistant and it got spread good. No one knew it in the White House." *

The President kept on in an unmodulated voice about "the great handicap" of the "disloyalty" and "unpatriotic sentiments of the Department of State. . . . It's gotten so that you can't have intercourse with your wife without it being spread around by traitors." He seemed angrier at what he called the "cheap press" than at the leak and he denounced the news reporting services for playing so prominently Eartha Kitt's angry exchange with Mrs. Johnson at a recent White House luncheon,** offering the incident as an example of what he meant.

More calmly, the President went on, saying that Rusk had worked on a speech for two months and "not even a quote" appeared in the newspapers. But the President had uppermost in his mind what *was* published and he was quickly back on the subject: "The Communists read all this." And he added: "The government is infiltrated and the airwaves are infiltrated." So, he said, in order to visit the Pope "I had to outsmart my own State Department and the Communists, too."

---

* I was startled by this apparent accusation against the probity of the faithful Rusk, but I was satisfied the President had meant to say that the information had been divulged somehow through the Secretary's unwitting agency.

** At that luncheon on January 18, to which fifty white and black women had been invited in order to discuss crime in the streets, Miss Kitt took the floor to assert that young people were rebelling and using marijuana because of the war in Vietnam. Mrs. Johnson—"her voice shaking and with tears in her eyes"—replied, "I'm sorry I do not understand the things that you do. I have not lived with the background that you have. . . . But I think we have made advances in these things and we will do more." (*The New York Times,* Jan. 19, 1968.)

He went on to talk about the theme of the conversations at the Vatican. He told the Pope that the United States would be glad to stop the bombing if the other side would not take advantage of the halt. "The problem was not with us. We'd deliver our share of the bargain if he could get the other side to deliver theirs." The President said parenthetically that the Pope "could exercise influence in South Vietnam" because the President and Vice-President there were Catholics. Then the President emphasized: "We are ready to do our full part." He said heatedly that the report that he and the Pope had had a dispute was absolutely false: "It didn't happen. We talked about Luci's conversion."

The President reached for a green leather photograph album containing pictures of his journey. Turning the pages he commented on each picture with animation. As we looked at a picture of him with troops, he said: "I couldn't be in that part of the world without being by my men." In a tone of irony he said, "Leonard Lyons and Joe Kraft* say I have no charisma, no popularity." As we looked at a picture of him pinning a medal on a bandaged black soldier lying in bed, he said: "You can imagine how that fellow must have felt being decorated by the President of the United States."

I asked the President why there was so much opposition in Congress to his Vietnam policy. "The moorings of it are in isolation," he replied. "A little of it is racism," he continued. "Some say the Vietnamese are not our kind of people. Very little of the opposition is based on good judgment." But because of the opposition, he maintained, "Hanoi is in better shape. . . . My weakness is in trying to protect the country." He then looked me squarely in the eye. "Who wants to yield to China and the Soviet Union?" he asked. "McCarthy," he went on, "agreed with the war when he wanted to be my vice-president. And no one hates war more than I do or my wife does or my mother did." He

* The syndicated columnists.

mentioned in an even voice that "Lynda's husband will soon be in Vietnam."

Now I asked a question that I had not had time to ask the last time we had talked. "Mr. President, do you ever have doubts about your policy?" Almost instantaneously he answered: "Yes, every decision you make, you have doubts about." "I listen to all sides constantly . . . I seek the preachers and the teachers," and he listed some of them: "Reischauer,* Gavin, Kennedy,** McGovern,† the Soviet Ambassador, the Polish Ambassador, Strom Thurmond,‡ Symington,§ the Joint Chiefs, and General Eisenhower." Naturally, he said, he "had to apply a lot of tests that other people don't have to apply." He talked of his critics again—like "Galbraith, who helps to prolong the war." He called them "simpletons." He described the commentators on the war as divided "between cut-and-run people and patriotic people."

We continued to discuss the opponents of Administration policy. He talked of the call to stop the bombing. "Well," he said, "they didn't object to throwing bombs on Hitler. Vietnam is just as precious a cargo as Israel." He mentioned the opposition of Senator Gruening‖ to the bombing—possibly because Gruening was Jewish—and he said, "I don't do it on the basis of how they spell their name." The "it" meant defense against aggression. "Most of them have set [sic] out all the wars," he asserted. "They love liberty but only talk about it. They have no style or character; they are uncouth and they have no guts. . . . McCarthy was not even

---

* Edwin O. Reischauer, University Professor at Harvard; former Ambassador to Japan, and a specialist on Asian affairs.
** Senator Robert F. Kennedy (Democrat, New York).
† Senator George S. McGovern (Democrat, South Dakota), a leading "dove."
‡ Republican Senator from South Carolina, a leading Southern voice.
§ Senator Stuart Symington (Democrat, Missouri), a former Secretary of the Air Force.
‖ Ernest Gruening (Democrat, Alaska).

in there against Hitler and Tojo: he was a very essential teacher." He snorted and with deep sarcasm said: "They have a real feeling for danger. They are eager beavers; they see a fire and they turn off the hose because it is essential that we not waste any water."

I posed another question I had never asked him before: "Do you visualize some precise sort of end to the war?" "Yes," he replied very quietly, but he declined to go beyond that single word and make any prediction. "I have to protect myself," he explained. And he recalled "how Bob Mc-Namara had predicted we would be out in 1965." The President said vehemently that that prediction was based on favorable conditions shortly changed by unforeseen events and that McNamara had unjustly been "branded a liar."

He harked back to his critics: "Fifteen to twenty percent of the people question everything about us. They engage in character assassination. They have none of the feeling for the independence of brown men that they have for people of their own race." Then, as if to sum up everything in a phrase, he set down some words on the picture which he had sent Jones for and which he meant to inscribe to me. As he wrote, he said: "It's the New Asia that I'm talking about." And the inscription read: "To Dr. Henry F. Graff, whose interest in the New Asia strengthens me."

The President called for a copy of *No Retreat from Tomorrow,* an elegantly printed and illustrated edition of his major messages to the 90th Congress. After inscribing it for me, he turned its pages and as he did, commented steadily on things uppermost in his thoughts, the elements of his Great Society programs. He pointed to a picture of himself with a very aged woman who was patting his cheeks with both her hands, and said, "The old folks. That's a dandy!" We looked at a picture of a gift of American grain arriving in India and he said mockingly: "Oil-rich Texans with no social consciousness." We looked at pictures of young people

151

with him. "They say I don't appeal to young people," he re-marked, his eyes narrowing. "That's a lot of crap. . . . There are a million and a quarter young people in schools who weren't there three years ago." As we continued to turn the pages, he said casually as if in comparison with himself: "Every time you look, Bobby Kennedy is being seen in a reform school or a Yeshiva." We went over picture after picture of Great Society accomplishments. At one point I asked him whether America could have both guns and but-ter; he closed the book, slapped it hard, and answered as he looked up at me: "*That's* whether you can or not."

DOMESTIC SPENDING

I then asked off-handedly how the war was affecting the domestic program. His answer was direct: "The cities are being used as an excuse by those who are against the war and the war is being used by the people who are against spending." He insisted, "We have the essentials for both if we have the will." Then he showed me on a chart in the book how the percentage of the Gross National Product being spent on the war each year was declining.

The President seemed to want to talk more even after an aide indicated to me that the allotted time was up. Again, the President detailed the unfairness of the criticism he was facing. "They are calling Clifford one of my 'cronies,' " he said, referring to Clark Clifford, his new Secretary of De-fense. "Why, I swear I have never spent forty minutes with him socially." "McCarthy in his balmiest days was not so bigoted," he said, referring this time to Joseph R. McCarthy, the late Senator from Wisconsin. When the President began to speak of "you professors," I demurred vigorously. He grinned and grasped me by the forearm. We said good-bye to each other and I thanked him for spending so much time with me.

☆ ☆ ☆ ☆ ☆ ☆

Before January, 1968 ended, the optimism of a few weeks earlier had given way to deep gloom. On January 22 the electronic intelligence ship, U.S.S. *Pueblo* was captured by North Korea while on patrol off the North Korean port of Wonsan. The President responded by calling to active duty 15,000 Air Force and Navy reservists. Moreover, he ordered the nuclear-powered aircraft carrier, *Enterprise,* to assume a station off the coast of South Korea. Even as he denounced the North Koreans' "wanton" act, he was keenly aware that because of the war in Vietnam he lacked freedom of action.

On Wednesday, January 31, while Saigon was celebrating the Lunar New Year, the Vietcong launched an attack on the city. By Friday, major assaults had been mounted on almost every significant city or provincial capital in South Vietnam. Although General Westmoreland said that the Tet Offensive—as it came to be known—had been expected, its size and its destructiveness apparently had not been. The attacks seemed to prove that despite the bombings in the North, the enemy could still concentrate and supply his troops. The attacks indicated, furthermore, that the work of pacification in the villages had not made a sufficient number of peasants loyal to the government at Saigon and, beyond that, that the cities themselves were not safe from attack.

When the Spring began, the President was continuing to lean heavily on his generals' assessment of the military prospects. As beleaguered Americans defended themselves at Khesanh, the President revealed to Congressmen and to the press that he had received written endorsement of the plans for the defense of Khesanh from each member of the Joint Chiefs of Staff. Khesanh seemed to symbolize the Administration's determination to stick it out in Vietnam. The President attempted to rally support in the nation by personally bidding farewell to a contingent of troops being hurried to the war zone. And General Westmoreland was reported to be seeking *another* 200,000 men for combat.

All the while, the hostility to the war mounted in Congress and outside, and the Senate Foreign Relations Committee in February was reexamining the basis for the Tonkin Gulf Resolution: the North Vietnamese "attack" on two American destroyers on the night of August 4, 1964.

The political scene reflected the deep feelings about the way the war was going. Senator Eugene McCarthy unexpectedly won the Democratic primary in New Hampshire and shortly afterward Senator Robert F. Kennedy decided to enter the race for the Presidency, too—both men making the Administration's policies in Vietnam the central point of their appeal for support. On Sunday, March 31, in a public address, President Johnson announced that he was calling a halt to the bombing of much of North Vietnam. And in a dramatic ending to the address he declared that he would not seek another term in the White House.

Soon thereafter the President recalled General Westmoreland to Washington and elevated him to be Army Chief of Staff. Westmoreland's successor in Vietnam was to be his deputy, General Creighton W. Abrams. In the meantime, Hanoi and Washington sparred over the choice of the site for preliminary talks between the United States and North Vietnam—finally agreeing on Paris.

The war seemed to have a life of its own independent of Presidential politics. By the Fall the talks in Paris, which began on May 13, had apparently bogged down badly, each side publicly vowing not to bow to the other's demands. Hanoi was insisting on an unconditional halt to the bombing of the North and Washington was insisting on reciprocity as a condition.

IV.

HALTING THE AIR ATTACKS ON THE NORTH

IN THE BEGINNING OF OCTOBER, 1968, THE WAY WAS BEING opened for a complete cessation of the bombing of the North. The Administration had worked out a formula under which the United States would halt the bombing as a step toward peace, expecting in return that the abuses of the demilitarized zone as well as Vietcong or North Vietnamese attacks on the cities or other populated areas would cease and that Hanoi would "enter promptly into serious political discussions that included the elected government of South Vietnam." The Administration over and over again reviewed the points with Ambassador W. Averell Harriman, its representative in Paris and his deputy, Cyrus R. Vance.

On October 9 at a regular meeting of the Americans and the North Vietnamese representatives, the Hanoi negotiators expressed interest in the proposals. Pointedly they asked whether America would halt the bombing if they agreed to permit the Saigon government to participate in the negotiations. As instructed, Harriman immediately pressed the other two points upon the North Vietnamese spokesmen, and promised to seek a reply from Washington. President Johnson was now faced with an extremely difficult decision. He conferred with General Abrams and with the United States Ambassador to South Vietnam, Ellsworth Bunker. Both men apparently were inclined to regard North Vietnam's inquiry as a favorable development, an indication that Hanoi would take the next step upon receiving an affirmative response.

This judgment of Abrams and Bunker fitted with a viewpoint they had already developed that the time had come to shift activities from the battlefield to the conference room. President Thieu, under pressure from Ambassador Bunker, accepted the idea of an affirmative answer to Hanoi. The Allied governments with troops deployed in Vietnam were also consulted and they assented to the proposal.

On October 14 President Johnson brought his senior advisers together at the White House to discuss Hanoi's démarche. Unanimously, it was reported, they approved of an affirmative reply. Almost immediately Harriman in Paris informed the Hanoi delegates of the positive decision taken in Washington and he reminded them of the conditions under which the bombing would have to be resumed. The first rejoinder of the North Vietnamese was to object to Harriman's insistence that expanded talks begin "the next day," choosing instead to speak of an interval of several weeks.

It was soon clear that Hanoi did not wish to regard these broadened talks as being only two-sided, with the United States and Saigon on one side and North Vietnam and the Vietcong on the other. They spoke rather of four-sided talks —a proposal not satisfactory to Washington at the time.

A concession was made to this last Hanoi demand, and agreement reached to halt the bombings and bring the Saigon and Vietcong spokesmen to Paris without going into the question of how they would be related to the principals. As to the conditions under which the bombing would be halted, Washington reported that Hanoi had given "reason to believe" that it understood the importance of restraining itself militarily, as the Administration was insisting. Before announcing the break in the logjam, the President sought personal assurance from General Abrams that the halt in the bombing would not jeopardize American lives in South Vietnam, and he called him home. On October 31 the President announced that as of 8 A.M. (Eastern Standard Time; 9 P.M. Vietnam Time) Friday, November 1, he was ordering a complete cessation of all United States air, naval, and artillery bombardment of North Vietnam. Almost immediately Saigon expressed resentment at apparently being put on the same footing with the Vietcong and announced that South Vietnam would not participate in the meetings at Paris.

On November 19, 1968

IN THE WEEK AFTER THE ELECTION, I WENT TO WASHINGTON and the White House again. I was making a study of the Presidential transition, and I wanted, in addition to doing research, to discuss with President Johnson's staff the details being worked out for the orderly transfer of the Presidency to Richard Nixon. I sensed, as others also could, that there was an unwonted spirit of relaxation in the Executive Offices. I had long before learned that the White House vibrated at fever pitch when the President was in town, but that the moment he left for other parts, a remarkable ease came over the staff—giving the impression of everybody in the building having simultaneously exhaled. Now, though the President was in the house, the tension was as gentle as if he were away: like a clock, his Administration was running down even though it ticked as strongly as before.

Before I left I called on George Christian. Good-humored and unhurried as usual, he said he hoped to be in touch with me shortly about a final visit with the President. The following week, sooner than I had dared to expect, Christian's secretary telephoned to invite me to the White House to be with the President at 5 P.M. on Tuesday, November 19. As I waited at LaGuardia Airport for the 3 P.M. "shuttle" plane, I chatted briefly with General Maxwell Taylor who, by coincidence, was also on the flight and standing ahead of me on line. As we boarded the aircraft, I remember thinking of the role he had played as Ambassador to South Vietnam and how the confident expectations of 1965 that he had helped voice had not yet been fulfilled. He looked tired and drawn.

When I arrived at the White House at about 4:30, I went to the Press Office where Christian said that the President would receive me and some others at five o'clock "in the Mansion." I was taken to the Diplomatic Reception Room, that elegant apartment which opens on the South Lawn, to wait for a few minutes. Its magnificent eighteenth-century wallpaper was chosen by Mrs. Jacqueline Kennedy when she was the First Lady. Seeing it among other signs of her passage, one could not fail to be keenly aware that the Kennedy-Johnson era had left positive marks of many kinds on the face of the world. The other guests were already there when I walked in: Marianne Means and Carl Rowan, the columnists; Saville Davis of the *Christian Science Monitor*; Peter Lisagor of the *Chicago Daily News,* and Eric Sevareid of the Columbia Broadcasting System. We exchanged small talk. Sevareid was the only one I had met before. Historians and journalists have more in common than they readily admit to each other—at least in their relationship to events. The difference, of course, is in the length of the perspective they prefer. At that moment, the subject did not seem one to talk about. It was sufficient that we were bound together willy-nilly by an invitation from the President of the United States.

In a few minutes we were ushered upstairs to the Yellow Oval Room to await the President. As we sat and talked, the warmth and beauty of the room engulfed us. Waiters moved about serving drinks and hors d'oeuvres. The conversation turned in part on the violence in the streets of Chicago during the recent Democratic convention, as Carl Rowan and Peter Lisagor offered especially vivid accounts of their experiences. The wait was longer than it seemed, perhaps, because the conversation stayed bright and political. At one point, one of the correspondents wondered—not seriously—whether the room was "bugged" and the President was listening in. Someone said he thought he had just seen George Washington wink; we all looked up at the Gilbert Stuart portrait hanging above the mantel.

We had sat for a good while when an usher came into the room to say that there was a call for me on the phone in the corridor. My heart turned over because I knew it must be a terrible emergency: only my wife knew where I was. But it was George Christian calling from the Press Office to ask if I expected to remain in Washington that night. I had no plans to stay over and told him so. He then invited me to fly back to New York with the President. The President, he explained, was going to address the Urban League. (Afterward, the President said, "Whitney Young was on the phone all day to get me to come.") I accepted at once. Christian asked me please not to say anything to the other guests because the President's intention to travel was not being announced.

Around seven the President strode into the room, sat down, and apologized for having kept us waiting. As I had noticed in the past was his habit, he opened his remarks with a reference to his previous appointment: he had been with Secretary Rusk just returned from Europe. Rusk "looks ill and tired. . . . We talked about the air bases in Spain," he said. "Spain is being difficult," he added, and then left the subject.

THIEU'S RESISTANCE

The President turned to the main topic of discussion. It was apparently going to be the bombing halt of October 30. The President began by expressing "sympathy and understanding for Thieu, as a fellow-President." Then he modulated to the subject of his critics. They were prepared, he said, to be excessively generous in making an offer to the other side. "Some of our beloved, well-intentioned Democratic friends screwed things up for two or three weeks just good and proper. I felt like saying 'Keep your big trap closed.' " He went on, "Well, we just were not gonna roll on those terms. What we said had to be met." This was shorthand to explain that the United States would not halt the bombing without some kind of agreement with Hanoi.

Thieu was understandably worried, the President said, because a withdrawal and a halt to the bombing would leave him without protection. That prospect "gave hope to Hanoi but it was frightening to South Vietnam." The President went on, without anyone interrupting: "Le Duk Tho [chief spokesman of North Vietnam in Paris] said he felt he had been misled and that he had to consult further with his government." In short, the President said without raising his voice, those suggestions from the sidelines made difficulties: they "rocked Thieu and got the Republicans agitated." The Republicans were announcing that "Johnson would sell out another China to elect Humphrey." They were saying that "I'm a wheeler-dealer." (Peter Lisagor interjected the word "tricky" and Johnson nodded in agreement.) They were asking: "Are you getting ready for a deal?"

And the same people, the President went on, "listed the things that 'I could not do, and get reelected. First was deal with the riots, second was deal with Vietnam, and the third was get a tax bill. The Republicans were saying that the Democrats would destroy the dollar to help Johnson get reelected. . . . Well, as Clarence Saunders used to say, 'I'm the sole owner of my name.'"

He was in a mood to flay the Republicans quite as much as to talk about the war. "They got nervous about how I was dealing with South Vietnam. They talked about 'sellout' and 'withdrawal.' The China lobby was busy. All the evil forces around town started rearing their ugly heads." Then, referring to his announcement of a halt in the bombing on the eve of the election, he said, "I hadn't picked the thirty-first of October in advance." (As he talked, Harry McPherson, his chief speechwriter, entered the room and the President stopped to say "Hello, Harry," motioning him to sit down.)

The President resumed: "A joint announcement was drafted and agreed upon. . . . Sunday, Hanoi had accepted while I was at the airport in New York. I had gone to New

York," he explained, "to speak to the ethnic groups with Humphrey.

"That night we tried to tie things down. . . . I was sensitive about the credibility charge. . . . I told Hanoi that discussions cannot be productive unless they are prompt." The discussions will be carried on "by your side and by our side. We offered to go tit for tat or even two tits for one tat." He paused for emphasis. "Bring your chauffeur if you care to," he reported we had told the negotiators. But he insisted that Hanoi agree to respect the DMZ and give up the shelling of the cities.

To be absolutely positive that the other side understood him on this, he continued, "I instructed Harriman twelve separate times to make sure. . . . When I asked him to make sure again, he was sore, but he told 'em again anyhow." Not to make absolutely certain, the President said, was like opening the way for "your wife to be attacked out in the hall." The President observed in a spirit of understanding rather than impatience, "Ky's doubts were unjustified." Bunker and Abrams urged him to accept the arrangement. About this, Johnson was matter of fact. "There is a great difference between August and October," he went on. General Abrams thought then that "hundreds of our men would be murdered" if we stopped the bombing. "I have two of my own there and I didn't want them murdered." The aim of ordering the halt was to "save us men." He talked of "the terrific losses" that the other side had suffered. "They've been defeated for several months," he explained, adding that "while they can still knock out a window-light [I took this to be a reference to terrorist activity], they have been out of it since September."

THE GENERALS' ASSESSMENT

At meetings with his advisers on the 13th, 14th, 15th, and 16th of October, the matter of a halt in the bombing was thrashed out. At one meeting with the Joint Chiefs lasting four hours, "I went down the line," he said, polling them on the question: "If you were the President would you stop the bombing?" All of them answered affirmatively, he said. He posed the question to others not present, too, including "Le May* men." They all agreed. "General Momyer was one of the strongest for stopping the bombing." **

The President continued to talk without interruptions. He said that before he acted he wanted an opinion in person from General Abrams. So he ordered Abrams to come home nonstop. (In an aside he said that Abrams had "stopped once —for re-fueling.") Abrams arrived at 2:30 A.M. on the 29th, and the President put to him the same question he had put to the other military leaders. Abrams, the President seemed eager to report, was the only one of them who replied, "It is presumptuous of me to answer the question." But, the President said, Abrams then went on, "As your field commander, I do urge you to take this action."

The President implied that Abrams agreed with the prevalent judgment that bombing was relatively valueless. The monsoon season had been on for ten days—unlike the circumstances that had obtained in August. "There are," said the President, "twenty-two hours of rain every twenty-four hours," and air action is only possible two days a month.

Then the President said, "We started putting Abrams to bed; he was exhausted from his trip. I hadn't even told Lady Bird that he was coming in," and "we had a job finding an empty room for him. . . . I woke up three maids looking for a room."

After that, the President said, "I went downstairs and joined Rusk and Rostow again. We had scrambled eggs and

* General Curtis E. LeMay (Retired), Chief of Staff of the Air Force from 1961 to 1965, was a vocal "hawk."
** Lieutenant-General William W. Momyer, the senior United States Air Commander in Vietnam.

coffee at the Cabinet Table." While eating, they received word that "Thieu had got unhitched" from the arrangement. The South Vietnamese did not want to appear dragooned to the peace table. They had (here the President was bitter), "assurances that I was a wheeler-dealer who would sell 'em out like China." So, the President continued, "we had to wake up Abrams and start again." Finally a phrase was agreed upon: the South Vietnamese "were free to come to the table." The President concluded soberly: "I hope and believe that Thieu will come and talk. We did not commit them to come. Bunker and Abrams are hopeful. But we will cross no bridges until we get to them. We will do what the national interest requires."

The President then stopped to ask for questions. He started with Marianne Means who asked about his relations with President-Elect Nixon. (She repeated her question after the President said, "A little louder, honey.") Johnson's tone in reply was eager. "Both of us are trying very hard; it's a strain on us to do what is best for the country. The less haggling and nitpicking the better. And it's good business for our grandchildren, too."

He enlarged: Nixon had asked to be briefed on international questions and an appointment was fixed immediately. Rusk, the President said, had done most of the talking at the resulting meeting. During its course, Rusk—"thoughtful Rusk," said the President—handed Nixon a paragraph the Secretary hoped to put into a speech he would deliver at the forthcoming NATO meeting. It was an invitation to NATO to hold its 20th Anniversary meeting in the United States in 1969 and Rusk wanted Nixon's approval because Nixon would be the President then. Nixon immediately assented. The President said he thought that this episode was what Nixon was referring to when he told newsmen in New York subsequently that his approval was being sought by the outgoing Administration. Why Nixon had said that—and obviously Johnson had been irritated—Johnson did not know. "I don't know why I say things myself," he said, and everybody laughed.

At the meeting with Nixon, Clark Clifford urged Nixon to select his [Clifford's] successor as soon as possible. Clifford had said on that occasion, "I will welcome him at staff meetings with the Joint Chiefs of Staff and the Secretaries. I hope he will be familiar with everything." The President continued, "Rostow and Bundy both felt that they came too late" to their post in the White House. And the President mentioned the Bay of Pigs as part of the price for the lateness. Rostow, said the President, told Nixon that he will welcome a successor and "take him as a brother." The President, switching to the matter of who those successors were likely to be—and sharing the curiosity of everyone in the room while trying to mask it, said casually, "It's hard to get qualified people. Nixon is going to be cautious."

The President went on talking about his conversations with Mr. Nixon and of his satisfaction at the cordiality that obtained. He spoke of the combination of "statesmanship and politics" that their meeting entailed. He said he thought the example "could be good for Saigon." Then, with amusement, he mentioned that his opponents had called him during the campaign "a crook, a thief, and a bank robber. Nixon didn't believe all that—not much!" He added that he had joked to Nixon: "I might sell you out."

Serious again, the President stated he had asked the President-elect to choose a representative to deal with foreign affairs. "He mentioned Mr. Murphy* and asked me to clear him with Rusk. . . . I told him I would be delighted with the choice of Murphy." After all, "I had tried him on the UN before I picked Ball. . . . I told Nixon I don't have to clear it with Rusk."

---

* Robert D. Murphy, a veteran diplomat who had ended a wide-ranging career in 1959 after serving as Undersecretary of State for Political Affairs.

The President said it was "just not true" that he had promised to seek Nixon's consultation and approval. [We saw above how the confusion may have arisen.] "I don't want to take a poll when the Russians get ready to launch missiles," he said sharply. "And I hope Hanoi doesn't think we are going to have a lottery to take a decision." "Some people," he said caustically, "think the President needs help with any decision from going to the bathroom to signing a treaty."

"Was Nixon consulted on the matter of ABM talks with Kosygin?" Peter Lisagor inquired. The President replied that he had been consulted. The President expressed the hope that he and Mr. Nixon would have the kind of friendly relation that Johnson had tried to maintain with General Eisenhower.

Now Carl Rowan asked Lyndon Johnson if he would make a forecast about the possible fate of Yugoslavia at the hands of the Soviet Union. The President replied that he would make no predictions and he reminded us of "the shape McNamara got in" when he had tried to make a prediction. The President added sternly, "I am concerned about the Soviets. They have a history of moving when they think they can get away with it."

The President was still thinking of them as he shifted the monologue to the transfer of power two months hence. "This is a dangerous period for us," he said. He revealed that President Eisenhower had said to John Kennedy on January 19, 1961: "You will have to move with men in Asia." For, the President went on, "missiles were moved in the period of the election." He was apparently referring to Soviet equipment and to the election just concluded.

U.S.–SOVIET RELATIONS

The difficulty and unpredictability of dealing with the Soviets now engrossed his mind. "Letters between us," he said, "have gone back and forth for four years." He was sure, he said, when he left Glassboro,* that progress on Vietnam and on anti-missile missiles would follow soon, that it would only be a short time before an anti-missile missile conference would be held—"perhaps the next week or next month." Eventually "the time and date and place were ready for announcement, but they moved into Czechoslovakia at seven o'clock the next night. The one thing I will never understand is why they didn't move while we were meeting. At least they would have made a boob out of me."

He returned to Rowan's question, saying the United States had bad intelligence on Romania and Yugoslavia and then added, "I don't want to speculate on what we'd do or have to do. How far do the American people want us to go to stop the Russian bear? How long are we willing to stay? How much sacrifice are we willing to make?"

Almost immediately he was back on the subject of Vietnam —and the American commitment. He spoke of the Tonkin Resolution. It had been copied, he said, from the Formosa Resolution, but a clause was added to do "whatever was necessary to deter" aggression. "SEATO," he said, "had been approved 83 to 1. I didn't sign it, Dirksen** didn't sign it, John Kennedy didn't sign it. But Mansfield signed it like John Hancock.† There was no need to rush passage of the Tonkin Gulf Resolution. They could have taken as much time on it as they took on Abe Fortas." ‡ His scorn was not to be

* The town and college in southern New Jersey where he had met with Premier Aleksei Kosygin in 1967.
** Senator Everett McKinley Dirksen (Republican, Illinois), the Minority Leader.
† Senator Mike Mansfield (Democrat, Montana), the Majority Leader. He had been a signatory of the Southeast Asia Treaty at Manila in September, 1954, in company with John Foster Dulles, then the Secretary of State, and H. Alexander Smith, then the senior Senator from New Jersey (Republican).
‡ In June, 1968, President Johnson had nominated his intimate friend Associate Justice Fortas of the Supreme Court to be Chief Justice. The nomination was never brought to a vote: after hearings before

mistaken. "Gruening and Morse were saying at that time," he continued like a debater, "that this could become a land war," implying that the possible consequences of the Resolution had been apparent to members of Congress. "But it passed by 504 to 2." He went on, "Russell says 'we're fickle,' " referring to Senator Richard Russell of Georgia, "so let them change it; they could do that any time by a simple resolution; they still can."

The President then talked about the Middle East. "Israel," he declared, "is our friend, and we'll defend it. President Kennedy made a campaign promise about that. I loved President Kennedy and I will support it."

Suddenly the President seemed more relaxed, as if having made the points he had intended to, he could now be free-wheeling in his comments. He spoke of the immediate future, in which he would be an ex-President. He said he would try to help the country from Johnson City. "At least I'm going to pray," he said, and once more everybody laughed. He was the partisan again as he said smiling, "Dick Nixon can't come into this room any too damn soon. I wish he was in here yesterday when we were discussing the franc."

As he talked on he shifted to his recollections of the troubles General Eisenhower had had to face in office. Johnson was obviously thinking of Latin America—and of his successor: "Nixon was the first Vice-President who had to be brought home from Venezuela by the Marines." There were troubles in Europe, too, he recalled: people were pressing Eisenhower "to issue an ultimatum on the Berlin question." Johnson added *en passant:* "Our intelligence did not justify issuing such an ultimatum."

At this point, the President nodded to Eric Sevareid to acknowledge a question. How big would the new budget be?

---

the Judiciary Committee and mounting criticism of Fortas' judicial ethics, it was apparent that confirmation would not be forthcoming. At the end of October, Fortas asked that his name be withdrawn.

The President replied that he was trying "to keep it at 186 billion." And he added that "the tax surcharge ought to be extended." He listed the new demands for money that were being made on him: "Everybody wants an increase. Clifford was in asking for six and a half billion more; Wilbur Cohen is asking for four and a half billion." With a ready memory for the figures, he recited the two billion more that Social Security would require, the four billion for federal pay increases and the billions for the highway-building program. Then he reminded us that Nixon had "twice said he was against the tax surcharge." The President wondered aloud where all the money was going to come from. "I just hope I can restrain my people's spending in the last month," he added in a mock-serious tone.

As everybody rose, he said to me, "You can ask me your questions on the plane."

Walking out of the room, the President preceding us, we were silent. I was taken again to the Diplomatic Reception Room. There a Secret Service man and a secretary were waiting to see me aboard the helicopter that was already whirring on the lawn outside. While we waited for the signal, Lynda Johnson Robb, clad in a bathrobe, walked by, wheeling her three-week-old baby. She stopped for a minute to allow us to admire the baby and I offered my congratulations. She said appealingly that she hoped no one would tell the nurse she had brought the baby down, but she wanted to see a movie being shown that evening. A second later, the word came for us to come aboard. "We have to hurry," said the secretary; "it will take off as soon as the President climbs in." We had just sat down when the President entered, wearing a modish silver-gray tuxedo with shawl collar. He seemed fresh and eager for the trip. W. Thomas Johnson, the Assistant Press Secretary, whose plan to return to Texas with the President after January 20 had already been announced, told him he could not find a paper the President had asked him for. The

President, slightly irritated, sent him back after telling him precisely which drawer it was in.

Meanwhile, the President handed me the reading copy of the speech he was going to deliver in New York.* Typed in oversize letters on large cards, it was a recital of the accomplishments of the Johnson Administration in the field of civil rights. "So," I said to him as Tom Johnson came aboard and we took off, "this is the summing up." Before the President could answer, the level of noise rose so that conversation became impossible. I continued to read the speech, and as I read I concluded that civil rights was the great sphere of achievement of the Administration, the bright side of the Johnson record. The war was the dark side. I surmised that after the session we had just had in the White House the President would prefer to talk about domestic affairs. He would want to dwell on what was congenial to him—and clearly his record at home filled the bill. But besides the noise of the motors as a hindrance to conversation, the lights were turned out as we gained altitude above the District of Columbia. We did not talk again during the few minutes it took to reach Andrews Air Force Base. A military honor guard snapped to attention as the helicopter landed a few yards from Air Force One, and the President alighted. In the darkness we walked quickly to the waiting plane.

President Johnson sat down in a seat facing forward; I opposite him. His valet set up a folding table between us and brought a tray of finger sandwiches: the President was going to meet Mrs. Johnson and some friends in New York for dinner later that night at the Hotel Pierre. We began to talk.

"Mr. President," I asked, "are there things you did in the White House that you wish you had done differently?" I hesitated to use the word "mistake," because I wanted to phrase

---

* The text is in *Public Papers of the Presidents of the United States: Lyndon B. Johnson, 1968–69,* Book II (Washington, D.C., 1970), pp. 1140–43.

my question exactly as I had put it to former President Truman when he visited Columbia University a number of years before. Such a question cannot, of course, be answered simply or briefly. But the character of the answer can be a clue in judging Presidential performance and in assessing the operations of power and decision-making. (Truman's response had been: "Anybody who's never made a mistake ought to put on his wings and get the hell out of here.") As the President answered, he fixed a somber gaze on me, squinting slightly as he said: "Yes, we've made mistakes." If foreign affairs were in his mind, he gave no sign. I asked him to be explicit. He must have been thinking of the home front and he had evidently given thought to the subject of self-evaluation: "We tried to do too much too quickly," as regards the Great Society programs. He described the difficulties in the administering of parts of it. He criticized Sargent Shriver, who had been the head of the war on poverty, for having "used the office to help Bobby Kennedy." His anger was unmistakable as he referred to the late Senator's book on the Cuban missile crisis about to be published posthumously.* "Ted Sorensen," he declared, "wrote that after Kennedy died."

Then he came back to the domestic scene. He felt keenly that his Administration had not adequately come to grips with "the problem of crime in the streets." He spoke of the anger that welled up in him "every time I hear of violence in the streets of Washington"—and of how furious it made him that his wife—and other women—could not go out at night and feel safe. He saw a relationship between the individual crimes against persons and the civil commotion in the country, for he immediately added that his Attorney General, Ramsey Clark, should have had "a big trial or two" in connection with the urban riots. He gave it as his opinion that it would have been "helpful to prosecute Stokely Carmichael."

* *Thirteen Days: A Memoir of the Cuban Missile Crisis.* New York: W. W. Norton and Company, 1969.

172

He did not specify the utility he had in mind, whether as help in dealing with urban problems or only as a political advantage.

Contemplating his return to private life, Johnson seemed to be facing south again politically. He speculated on "the cost of my program to 11 states and 22 men"—which I took to be a wistful reference to his native section and to its Senatorial contingent, both affected by the permanent changes he had been instrumental in fashioning. Then he summed up his enormous labors with crisp decisiveness: "I am well satisfied."

He talked of his return to Texas, of the Johnson Library, and of the support for it he was receiving. He mentioned in passing the generous contributions that had come in and he was specific about the help of "many Jewish friends." The President appeared serene and in good spirits, apparently feeling relief as well as pride. He spoke of his means in retirement. "They say I have millions but that's not so. I'm worth $400,000—enough to take care of me and my family."

The concern uppermost in his mind was his plan to lecture on college campuses in the months after leaving office. He had the intention of lecturing on a variety of subjects, including education and civil rights. He knew that he was challenging himself in a new way, being aware that the campuses of the country were no longer places where dutiful audiences could be expected as a matter of course to welcome an ex-President of the United States. "Dr. Graff, will you help me write those lectures?" he asked. I was startled by the bluntness of the request. I said yes, but hoped as I said it (and as I repeated in a memorandum-letter to one of his aides shortly afterward) that he could be persuaded to lecture not on the subjects he had enumerated, but on his understanding and handling of half a dozen major decisions he had taken in his years in the White House.

Continued student unrest quickly made his plans unwork-

173

able. I had no doubt, however, that the possibility of spending time on campuses enormously appealed to him. He asked me about the crisis at Columbia in the Spring of 1968 and, particularly, of the role played by Vice-President David B. Truman there. I quipped, "Mr. President, you know all about the trouble that Vice-Presidents have." He did not appear to hear me. (I understood that the possibility of Columbia's Truman being invited to be a professor at the University of Texas in connection with the Johnson Library and School there was in the President's mind.)

We were nearing LaGuardia Airport now and I knew we would land very shortly: the President of the United States is never kept waiting in the "stack." The President's valet came up to apply pancake makeup to the President's face in preparation for the television cameras. Tom Johnson inquired if I would care to join the Presidential party to hear the President deliver the address. I declined rather than further impose on his hospitality. The plane landed smoothly and the President and I bade each other goodbye; we would be in touch again, he hoped.

By the time I stepped out of the plane a few seconds later, the President was in his limousine and it was already on its way. I walked toward a police lieutenant to ask him how I could get to the Eastern Shuttle parking-lot, where I had left my car. He called to a sergeant: "Get this man wheels." In a few minutes I was at my car, feeling I had been delivered there by the power of the Presidency itself.

EPILOGUE

IN SPITE OF THE ACKNOWLEDGED BRILLIANCE OF THE TUESDAY Cabinet and their determination, when Lyndon B. Johnson left office on January 20, 1969, his prodigious efforts had brought neither peace nor victory in Vietnam. The mounting opposition to the war, making it practically impossible for the President or members of the Tuesday Cabinet to appear at public gatherings, expressed a lack of confidence in American leadership that neither the defeat at Brandywine nor the disaster at Chancellorsville had aroused on the home front in earlier days of national woe.

The crisis centered not on the terrible yet far more manageable matter of a threat to the nation's life, but on whether or not Americans were being led in actions foreign to the spirit of American democracy, that is, whether they ought to be in Vietnam at all. And for millions of Americans the lengthening of the war added to this issue the question of the integrity and intelligence of the President himself. Notwithstanding the reasons Johnson gave to the nation in March, 1968, for not seeking another term as President— that he was stepping aside in order to remove himself as a possible impediment to peace—many of his fellow-citizens will always maintain that the Johnson government "fell" as surely as if the United States were governed under a parliamentary system.

In the account I have given of conversations sought by the President and recorded in the spirit of sympathy without partisanship, the reader should have found not explanations for the failure of the President to produce in Vietnam the results he and most of his countrymen expected and wanted, but rather insights into how America's leaders from 1965 to 1969 continued to support and justify policies whose upshot dismayed them more and more. The reader should also have found here an image of the atmosphere in which the President and his advisers interacted, a sense of the complexity of their successive medicaments and a truer sense of the loyalty with which the men around the President defended him and the decisions they had helped him reach, regardless of any private misgivings they may have increasingly entertained.

The reader will moreover have noted afresh how national history and passion about current events commingle in unpredictable ways that add to the burdens and mysteries involved in conducting a war and governing a nation. Indeed, the reader cannot have failed to rediscover in these pages the evidences of the wearing loneliness that shrouds the center of governmental power. That loneliness proceeds from the daily recognition that there is no answerbook for the problems demanding solutions and that the consequences of choosing one option rather than another are irreversible.

The reader has no need to be told that President Johnson was not an especially articulate man. Had he been so, he would have exercised directly on the people his considerable gift for persuasion, which was often so effective in private. Yet not even one who perceives how his fiery and often outrageous language put limits on his accomplishments, in a manner and to a degree that he only vaguely suspected, can be sure that articulateness was a vital missing element in his conduct of Vietnam affairs. And no one can mistake the truth that Johnson, using the best words at his command— the strong ones and sometimes the mean ones that he brought to Washington from the Pedernales Valley—was the undisputed leader in his official household. The leadership he exercised on his chief aides was demanding to an uncommon extent, and it sometimes made them seem submissive and peevish. He made his people his own and battened on them devouringly—with scowl and gesture as well as with words. Even when his men disagreed with him thoroughly he kept them aboard his ship, and they sailed uncomplainingly the way he charted the course. To resign from office over differences respecting policy has become an almost extinct political act in our day, a fact of which Johnson repeatedly took advantage.

The controls that operated on Johnson himself are not as readily discerned. A domineering man, he misgauged the length of time it would take for the operation of his policies to satisfy the general public he counted upon—possibly because he never ceased to think that he could will for America the outcome he sought in Asia. Yet, despite what some of his critics believed and said, he was not an autocrat deaf to suggestion and opposition. The most important control playing on Johnson he may have understood better than he ever could say: the one imposed on him by being President of the United States in his particular place in the line of the Presidents. If Lyndon Johnson could speak as he did of how he "walked with Lincoln every night," the truth was that he walked with all of his predecessors all the time. They guided him and limited him in a thousand ways, despite his personal style and his independence of mind and spirit.

Americans have only one President at a time, Johnson liked to remind people, but the Presidency, like other institutions, replicates its leadership willy-nilly. The office and its immense responsibilities inexorably capture the men who occupy it—together with their aides—and force them to express the same sentiments in similar words. Changes in costume and accent and physical appearance invest the office with drama and sustain the public's inquisitive attention. Yet the same man stands there decade after decade. Viewed from this standpoint, the utterances of Johnson and his ad-

179

visers, despite their speciality, have the quality of echoes out of the past. The utterances are Presidential, not merely Johnsonian.

Does one not hear in Johnson's words President Polk angered by criticisms of his management of affairs and confiding his wish that "friends in Congress and elsewhere would suffer me to conduct the war with Mexico as I thought proper; and not plan the campaign for me." Or the voice of James Madison declaring, during the War of 1812, that the American people will "cheerfully and proudly bear every burden of every kind which the safety and honor of the nation demand." Again, when Rusk shows testiness and scorn toward his critics, is it not the echo of his predecessor in the Department of State, William H. Seward—also of New York —writing to his daughter in 1862: "It is a startling sight to see the mind of a great people, saddened, angered, soured, all at once, and it is a painful thing to have all its anger, its fear, its uncharitableness poured, without reserve, into your own heart."

The people—and not only their Presidents and other leaders—become contemporaries of all those who have gone before them. In a great measure this is because the perspective of American history has been flattened by television, the motion pictures, illustrated histories, "restorations" of historical sites, and good history-writing. Public figures to a greater degree than ever in the past feel at one with their predecessors, and meet the ordeals of their office with extreme self-consciousness. The members of the Tuesday Cabinet (and by no means the ex-academics alone) alluded frequently and spontaneously to the past, going beyond whatever the requirement of courtesy may be in talking to a professional historian. It would be wrong to regard this phenomenon as superficial. History offers models to Presidents and their men, as it does to all people, and they cut their acts as well as their words according to the pattern of the heroes, the clichés, the striking events they fix on during formative years.

Politics imitates history, indeed, just as life imitates art. Johnson and his men went to school to the foreign policy of Franklin Roosevelt and Harry Truman and it stamped them indelibly: there they learned the value of firmness in conducting international relations, the price that unopposed military aggression must in the long run claim from all peaceful peoples, and the usefulness of lofty rhetoric in expounding foreign policies to a public that tends to think all wars avoidable. But the study of history can be misleading as well as instructive; for untrained minds, it too often simplifies rather than clarifies. Whatever else the members of the Tuesday Cabinet added to their knowledge in their time in office, they must have discovered (if they did not already know it) that public servants can be ensnared as well as inspirited by the past, even as they strive to build freshly upon it.

The decisions that Lyndon Johnson and his men reached in the Tuesday Cabinet are a fair target for historians and for the public at large, because the effects will continue to sear the pages on which the history of the twentieth century is to be written. The conversations recounted here are a portion of the evidence on which judgment will be rendered from time to time as the angle of vision narrows. The reader of this book now or years from now should understand that the men of the Tuesday Cabinet were strong, discerning, and gallant. That they were not able to bring about a clear-cut and favorable decision in Vietnam will raise questions about the means of implementing even the most exalted of national principles. Some readers will speculate afresh about the historical luck that turns some Presidential Administrations into marble monuments and others into contemptible ruins. Still others will settle the merits of the hypotheses that guided American leaders in the second half of the 1960's.

181

In any event and for any purpose, the reader of today and tomorrow has an obligation to remember that the words in these conversations were spoken by ordinary mortals. The members of the Tuesday Cabinet were neither mere amanuenses of events beyond their control, nor were they clairvoyants, able at will to lift the veil of the future. They should accordingly not be judged by the yardstick of qualifications that they did not have—and no men possess. They must be judged today, and in times to come, as men who believed deeply in the political system that produced them, the cultural inheritance that nourished them, and the usefulness of the light and succor that American idealism and materialism can offer the world. They never constituted that fancied company of Solons who unerringly would have confronted the tragic challenge of Vietnam with full comprehension and perfect wisdom.

APPENDIX

A. Members of the Tuesday Cabinet

B. Hanoi's Four Points

C. Washington's Fourteen Points

D. Washington's Peace Overtures

A. Members of the Tuesday Cabinet

MC GEORGE BUNDY, Special Assistant to the President for National Security Affairs, occupying that position from 1961 to 1966. Born in Boston in 1919, Bundy was graduated from Yale in 1940; during the Second World War, he served as an army officer in signal intelligence work. Subsequently, he joined the Harvard faculty as a member of the Department of Government and in 1953 was named Dean of the Faculty of Arts and Sciences. Bundy, who long had been a registered Republican, left Harvard in 1961 to join the Kennedy Administration. He resigned his position at the White House in 1966 in order to become President of the Ford Foundation. He was succeeded in the Tuesday Cabinet by Walt W. Rostow.

GEORGE EASTLAND CHRISTIAN, Special Assistant to the President and Press Secretary from 1966 to 1969. He was born in Austin, Texas in 1927. During the Second World War, he enrolled at the University of Texas, but interrupted his studies in order to join the Marines. In 1949 he entered the newspaper field as a sports editor for the Temple (Texas) *Daily Telegram*. Almost immediately, he moved to the International News Service as a correspondent. From 1956 to 1963, he was assistant to Price Daniel, then a Senator and shortly to be Governor of Texas. When Daniel left the governorship, Christian became assistant to his successor, John Connally.

184

CLARK MC ADAMS CLIFFORD, Secretary of Defense from 1968 to 1969. Born in Fort Scott, Kansas in 1906, he took a law degree at Washington University in St. Louis in 1928. He commenced private practice in St. Louis upon graduation, developing specialties in corporation and labor law. During the Second World War he served as a naval officer, and in 1946 he was Naval Aide to President Truman. For the next four years, he served as Special Counsel to Truman. Subsequently, Clifford practiced law as the senior partner of a Washington firm. Without an official position, he was on close terms with Presidents Kennedy and Johnson who frequently sought his confidential advice.

RICHARD MC GARRAH HELMS, Director of the Central Intelligence Agency from 1966 on. He was born in St. Davids, Pennsylvania in 1913. After being graduated from Williams College in 1935 he went to Europe as a staff correspondent for the United Press; afterwards he was with the Indianapolis *Times*. During the Second World War, he was a naval officer and served with the Office of Strategic Services. In 1947, he joined the Central Intelligence Agency, then being organized.

ROBERT STRANGE MC NAMARA, Secretary of Defense from 1961 to 1968. Born in San Francisco in 1916, he was graduated in 1937 from the University of California at Berkeley. Upon receiving the M.B.A. degree from Harvard, he accepted an appointment there as an assistant professor of business administration. He remained until 1943, when he left to become an Air Force officer. After the war, he commenced a career as an executive of the Ford Motor Company, becoming its president in November, 1960, the first to have that position who was not a member of the Ford family. He had held the office for about a month when President Kennedy invited him to be head of the Department of Defense. He left the Defense Department in 1968 to become president of the World Bank. He was succeeded in the Tuesday Cabinet by Clark M. Clifford.

BILL D. MOYERS, Special Assistant to the President from 1963 to 1967 and Press Secretary from 1965 to 1967. Born in Hugo, Oklahoma in 1934, he was graduated from the University of Texas with a degree in journalism in 1956. The following year he was a student at the University of Edinburgh. Returning to the United States, he took a divinity degree in 1959, and was ordained a minister. Almost immediately, he became personal assistant to Senator Lyndon B. Johnson and during the Vice-Presidential campaign of 1960, he was Johnson's executive assistant. After the election, Moyers was associate director and subsequently deputy director of the Peace Corps, until Johnson's accession to the Presidency. In 1967, Moyers left the White House to become the publisher of *Newsday*, a Long Island (New York) daily newspaper. He was succeeded in the Tuesday Cabinet by George E. Christian.

WALT WHITMAN ROSTOW was Special Assistant to the President for National Security Affairs from 1966 to 1969. He was born in New York City in 1916; after being graduated from Yale in 1936, he spent the next two years as a Rhodes scholar at Balliol College, Oxford University. In 1940, he started an academic career at Columbia as an instructor in economic history. In 1946–47 and 1949–50, he held two prestigious professorships of American history in England. He was professor of economic history at the Massachusetts Institute of Technology from 1950 to 1960. In 1961, Rostow served under McGeorge Bundy as Deputy Special Assistant to the President for National Security Affairs before moving to the Department of State as Chairman of the Policy Planning

Council. When Bundy left the White House in 1966, Rostow succeeded him, and joined the Tuesday Cabinet.

DEAN RUSK, Secretary of State from 1961 to 1969. Born in Cherokee County, Georgia in 1909, he took an A.B. degree from Davidson College in North Carolina in 1931 and then studied as a Rhodes scholar at St. John's College, Oxford University. Returning to the United States, he was a professor of government and Dean of the Faculty at Mills College in Oakland, California, remaining there until 1940. After service in the Army as an officer in the Second World War, he entered the Department of State in 1946, his duties involving chiefly United States' international security affairs. In 1950, he became the Assistant Secretary of State for Far Eastern Affairs and played a significant part in the making of decisions that led to United States participation in the Korean War. He left State in 1952 to become president of the Rockefeller Foundation, remaining in that position until 1960 when President-elect Kennedy designated him to be his ranking Cabinet officer.

EARLE GILMORE WHEELER, Chairman of the Joint Chiefs of Staff from 1964 on. Born in Washington, D.C., in 1908, Wheeler was commissioned a second lieutenant of infantry in 1932 upon his graduation from the United States Military Academy at West Point. He rose through the grades to general in 1962, when he was appointed Army Chief of Staff by President Kennedy. During the Second World War, he was chief of staff of the 63rd Infantry Division. He held staff positions of increasingly greater responsibility from 1955 on and two major positions of command in the field: commanding general of the Second Armored Division and Deputy Commander-in-Chief of the United States European Command.

B. Hanoi's Four Points*

1. Recognition of the basic national rights of the Vietnamese people—peace, independence, sovereignty, unity, and territorial integrity. According to the Geneva agreements, the U.S. Government must withdraw from South Vietnam U.S. troops, military personnel, and weapons of all kinds, dismantle all U.S. military bases there, and cancel its military alliance with South Vietnam. It must end its policy of intervention and aggression in South Vietnam. According to the Geneva agreements, the U.S. Government must stop its acts of war against North Vietnam and completely cease all encroachments on the territory and sovereignty of the DRV [Democratic Republic of Vietnam].

2. Pending the peaceful reunification of Vietnam, while Vietnam is still temporarily divided into two zones, the military provisions of the 1954 Geneva agreements on Vietnam must be strictly respected. The two zones must refrain from entering into any military alliance with foreign countries and there must be no foreign military bases, troops, or military personnel in their respective territory.

3. The internal affairs of South Vietnam must be settled by the South Vietnamese people themselves in accordance

* From report of Premier Pham Van Dong, April 8, 1965, as transmitted by Radio Hanoi, April 13, 1965 (*The New York Times,* April 14, 1965).

with the program of the NLFSV [National Liberation Front of South Vietnam] without any foreign interference.

4. The peaceful reunification of Vietnam is to be settled by the Vietnamese people in both zones, without any foreign interference.

C. Washington's Fourteen Points*

1. The Geneva Agreements of 1954 and 1962 are an adequate basis for peace in Southeast Asia;

2. We would welcome a conference on Southeast Asia or on any part thereof;

3. We would welcome "negotiations without preconditions" as the 17 nations put it;

4. We would welcome unconditional discussions as President Johnson put it;

5. A cessation of hostilities could be the first order of business at a conference or could be the subject of preliminary discussions;

6. Hanoi's four points could be discussed along with other points which others might wish to propose;

7. We want no U.S. bases in Southeast Asia;

* From *Department of State Bulletin,* January 24, 1966, p. 116.

8. We do not desire to retain U.S. troops in South Vietnam after peace is assured;

9. We support free elections in South Vietnam to give the South Vietnamese a government of their own choice;

10. The question of reunification of Vietnam should be determined by the Vietnamese through their own free decision;

11. The countries of Southeast Asia can be non-aligned or neutral if that be their option;

12. We would much prefer to use our resources for the economic reconstruction of Southeast Asia than in war. If there is peace, North Vietnam could participate in a regional effort to which we would be prepared to contribute at least one billion dollars;

13. The President has said, "The Vietcong would not have difficulty being represented and having their views represented if for a moment Hanoi decided she wanted to cease aggression. I don't think that would be an insurmountable problem."

14. We have said publicly and privately that we could stop the bombing of North Vietnam as a step toward peace although there has not been the slightest hint or suggestion from the other side as to what they would do if the bombing stopped.

D. Washington's Peace Overtures
Negotiation Attempts on Vietnam*

April 7, 1965: President Johnson stated that the U.S. was prepared to enter into "unconditional discussions" with the other governments concerned in the Vietnam problem.

May 13–17, 1965: The U.S. suspended its bombing operations against North Vietnam. This suspension was made known to the other side to see if there might be a response in kind.

June 25, 1965: President Johnson called upon members of the UN, "individually and collectively to bring to the table those who seem determined to make war. We will support your efforts, as we support effective action by any agent or agency of these United Nations."

June 28, 1965: President Johnson, in a letter to UN Secretary General U Thant, reiterated his hope that "members of the UN, individually and collectively, will use their influence to bring to the negotiating table all governments involved in an attempt to halt all aggression and evolve a peaceful solution."

July 30, 1965: In a letter to the UN Security Council President, Ambassador Goldberg noted that responsibility to persist in the search for peace weighs especially upon members of the Security Council. He stated that the U.S. stands ready, as in the past, to collaborate unconditionally with members of the Security Council in the search for an acceptable formula to restore peace and security in Southeast Asia.

January, 1966: The U.S. continued until January 31 the pause in the bombing of North Vietnam initiated at Christmas, and dis-

* From an unofficial compilation by the Bureau of East Asian and Pacific Affairs of the Department of State, originally prepared January 6, 1967. The abridgement printed here does not include proposals by third parties that the U.S. approved of or encouraged.

patched Governors Harriman and Williams and Ambassador Goldberg on missions to seek diplomatic channels to Hanoi for negotiations and to explain the U.S. position.

January 31, 1966: Ambassador Goldberg sent a letter to Security Council President Matsui, summarizing the U.S. position on negotiations and requesting an urgent meeting of the Security Council to consider the Vietnam situation.

April 18, 1966: Senator Mansfield proposed that the U.S., Hanoi, and "elements in South Vietnam" meet at a peace conference in some Asian country. The White House and the Department of State endorsed the Mansfield proposal.

December 19, 1966: Ambassador Goldberg sent a letter to UN Secretary General U Thant which referred to Pope Paul's appeal that the temporary Christmas truce be transformed into a cessation of hostilities which would become the occasion for sincere negotiations. Ambassador Goldberg requested that the Secretary General take whatever steps he considered necessary "to bring about the necessary discussions" which could lead to such a ceasefire. The letter contained an assurance that the U.S. Government would cooperate fully with the Secretary General in getting such discussions started promptly and bringing them to a successful completion.

February 8–13, 1967: During the Tet (Lunar New Year) truce, the U.S. suspended bombing for 5 days and 18 hours after many weeks in which the U.S. Government had communicated to Hanoi several possible routes to peace, any one of which the U.S. was prepared to take. Four U.S. messages were sent to Hanoi in January and early February. On February 8 President Johnson wrote DRV President Ho Chi Minh and proposed to order the cessation of bombing against North Vietnam and the halt of further augmentation of U.S. forces in South Vietnam as soon as he was assured that infiltration into South Vietnam by land and sea had stopped. The President observed that these actions of restraint on both sides would make it possible to conduct serious and private discussions leading toward an early peace.

May 23–24, 1967: The U.S. and Government of Vietnam declared a 24-hour ceasefire affecting hostilities in both North and South Vietnam in order to observe Buddha's birthday, and in the hope that this would lead to a constructive response. Hanoi and the Vietcong refused to observe the ceasefire.

September, 1967: The U.S. again explored the possibility of Security Council action with members of the Council, suggesting five points as principles which it believed the Security Council might endorse in seeking a settlement based on the Geneva Accords.

September 2, 1967: Ambassador Goldberg again asked whether North Vietnam conceives that the cessation of bombing should lead to any other results than meaningful negotiation under circumstances which would not disadvantage either side. Ambassador Goldberg also asked how Hanoi's supporters would use their influence and power to move the Vietnam conflict promptly toward a peaceful solution, if we were to take the first step.

September 29, 1967: The President stated in his San Antonio speech that our desire to negotiate peace—through the United Nations or out—has been made very clear to Hanoi, directly and through third parties. President Johnson declared: "As we have told Hanoi time and time and time again the heart of the matter really is this: The United States is willing to stop all aerial and naval bombardments of North Vietnam when this will lead promptly to productive discussions. We, of course, assume that while discussions proceed, North Vietnam would not take advantage of the bombing cessation or limitation."

December 19, 1967: In his December 19, 1967 television interview with correspondents of ABC, CBS, and NBC, the President set forth five points as the basis of a solution in South Vietnam:

1. "The Demilitarized Zone must be respected as the 1954 Agreements require."
2. "The unity of Vietnam . . . must be a matter for peaceful adjustment and negotiation."
3. "The North Vietnamese forces must get out of Laos and stop infiltrating Laos. That is what the 1962 Agreements required, and it must be respected."
4. "The overwhelming majority of the people of South Vietnam want a one man-one vote constitutional government."
5. "President Thieu has said . . . that he is prepared for informal talks with members of the NLF and that these could bring good results. I think that is a statesmanlike position. And I hope the other side will respond."

January 25, 1968: Secretary of Defense-Designate Clark Clifford, testifying before the Senate Armed Services Committee, said that he would "expect to follow the language of the President" where Mr. Johnson has stated that if the North Vietnamese would agree to start negotiations promptly and not take advantage of a pause in bombing, the U.S. would stop its air and sea bombardment. Mr. Clifford, in replying to a question from Senator Thurmond, said that he did not expect the North Vietnamese to stop their military activities prior to an agreed ceasefire and that he assumed "that they will continue to transport the normal amount of goods, munitions, and men to South Vietnam."

Proposed First
Steps toward Peace*

1. A reconvening of the Geneva conference of 1954 and a return to the agreements of 1954.
2. A reconvening of the Geneva conference of 1962 on Laos and a return to the agreements of 1962.
3. A conference on Cambodia.
4. An all-Asian peace conference.
5. A special effort by the two cochairmen, Britain and the Soviet Union, to approach the two sides for a peaceful settlement.
6. A special effort by the International Control Commission—India, Canada, Poland—to probe the two sides for a peaceful settlement.
7. A role for the U.N., the Security Council, the General Assembly, the Secretary-General.
8. Talks through intermediaries, either singly or as a group.
9. Direct talks either with the Government of South Vietnam or with the U.S.
10. An exchange of prisoners of war.

* From Secretary Rusk's remarks at a White House luncheon for General Westmoreland on April 28, 1967. Rusk introduced the list as representing "the proposals which we and other governments have made pointing toward peace in Southeast Asia during the past 2 or 3 years. . . . [O]n each of these we have said yes, and on each of these Hanoi has said no." *Public Papers of the Presidents of the United States: Lyndon B. Johnson, 1967*, Book I (Washington, 1968), pp. 475–6.

11. The supervision of the treatment of prisoners by the International Red Cross.

12. Demilitarize the DMZ.

13. Or widen and demilitarize the DMZ.

14. The interposition of international forces between the combatants.

15. The mutual withdrawal of foreign forces including the forces of North Vietnam from South Vietnam.

16. Assistance to Cambodia to assure its neutrality and territory.

17. The cessation of bombing linked with the stop of infiltration.

18. A cessation of the augmentation of U.S. forces.

19. Three suspensions of bombings in order to permit serious talks.

20. The discussion of Hanoi's Four Points along with whatever points others might raise, such as Saigon's Four Points and our own Fourteen Points.

21. Or discussion of an agreed four points as a basis for negotiation.

22. A willingness to find the means to have the views of the Liberation Front heard in peace discussions.

23. Negotiations without conditions, negotiations about conditions, or private discussions about a final settlement.

24. If peace, then the inclusion of North Vietnam in a large development program for all of Southeast Asia, including North Vietnam.

25. The Government of South Vietnam to be determined by free elections among the people of South Vietnam.

26. The question of reunification to be determined by free elections among the peoples of both South Vietnam and North Vietnam.

27. Reconciliation with the Vietcong and readmission of its members to the body politic of South Vietnam.

28. And South Vietnam's ability to be neutral in the future, if it so chooses.

Index